Talent Management

Talent management is a central element of managerial discourse and organisational practice. This short-form book provides a succinct overview on the state of research on talent management.

The authors set out the key themes, arguments, trends and future research trajectories of talent management, highlighting major works in the field. As a research topic with a fragmented body of knowledge, pluralistic perspectives are summarised, while workforce differentiation emerges as a central element.

A critical introduction for students, scholars and reflective practitioners, this book guides readers through a relatively new and rapidly developing area of management research.

Anthony McDonnell is Full Professor of Human Resource Management and Head of the Department of Management and Marketing at the Cork University Business School, University College, Cork, Ireland. He has held appointments at Queen's University Belfast, University of South Australia and University of Newcastle, Australia. His research has been funded by the Australian and Irish Research Councils and Ireland Canada University Foundation.

Sharna Wiblen is Assistant Professor at the Sydney Business School, University of Wollongong, Australia. Sharna blends academic skills and 15 years of industry experience including time as a management consultant, human resource and recruitment coordinator, and retail service manager to broker dialogue between academics and industry to advance the study and practice of responsible talent management.

State of the Art in Business Research
Series Editor: Geoffrey Wood

Recent advances in theory, methods and applied knowledge (alongside structural changes in the global economic ecosystem) have presented researchers with challenges in seeking to stay abreast of their fields and navigate new scholarly terrains.

State of the Art in Business Research presents shortform books which provide an expert map to guide readers through new and rapidly evolving areas of research. Each title will provide an overview of the area, a guide to the key literature and theories and time-saving summaries of how theory interacts with practice.

As a collection, these books provide a library of theoretical and conceptual insights, and exposure to novel research tools and applied knowledge, that aid and facilitate in defining the state of the art, as a foundation stone for a new generation of research.

Titles in the series include:

Operations Management
A Research Overview
Michael A. Lewis

Work and Stress
A Research Overview
Philip Dewe and Cary L Cooper

Management Gurus
A Research Overview
David Collins

Talent Management
A Research Overview
Anthony McDonnell and Sharna Wiblen

For more information about this series, please visit: www.routledge.com/

Talent Management
A Research Overview

**Anthony McDonnell
and Sharna Wiblen**

Routledge
Taylor & Francis Group

LONDON AND NEW YORK

First published 2021
by Routledge
2 Park Square, Milton Park, Abingdon, Oxon OX14 4RN

and by Routledge
52 Vanderbilt Avenue, New York, NY 10017

Routledge is an imprint of the Taylor & Francis Group, an informa business

© 2021 Anthony McDonnell & Sharna Wiblen

The right of Anthony McDonnell & Sharna Wiblen to be identified as authors of this work has been asserted by them in accordance with sections 77 and 78 of the Copyright, Designs and Patents Act 1988.

British Library Cataloguing-in-Publication Data
A catalogue record for this book is available from the British Library

Library of Congress Cataloging-in-Publication Data
A catalog record for this book has been requested

ISBN: 978-0-367-35863-1 (hbk)
ISBN: 978-0-367-68446-4 (pbk)
ISBN: 978-0-429-34230-1 (ebk)

DOI: 10.4324/9780429342301

Typeset in Times New Roman by
Apex CoVantage, LLC

Anthony

To Therese and Tess. You represent fully what is important and valuable to me.

Sharna

To Robbie, Emmett, Sierra and Jenson who are always on my team and forever reminding me that while the words I write are valuable because they contribute to knowledge – it is the words I share with them, every day, that have the most significant impact.

To talent management advocates – existing, new and forthcoming – together, we shall learn about and #talkabouttalent because talent management is a team sport.

Contents

Tables

1 Talent management

An introduction

Introduction

This book provides a succinct overview on the state of research on talent management. Its short-form nature means that the focus is on providing a critical synopsis of what we see as the key themes, arguments, trends and future research trajectories. In so doing, we articulate the key publications within this field of research since its origins. As such, this book is likely to be of interest to students, scholars and professionals who want an overview of talent management as a research field. Our focus here is on internal talent management, although external hiring is often a key strategy used to fill talent needs.

It is not possible to identify a precise and agreed meaning of talent management given the varied definitions and assumptions that are evident in the literature (Lewis & Heckman, 2006). However, talent management has become increasingly seen as referring to how organisations anticipate and meet their talent needs for the most strategically important roles. The rise of talent management as a discrete research field is typically traced to the McKinsey Company's talk of major talent shortages and the emotive language of the 'war for talent' (Chambers, Foulon, Handfield-Jones & Michaels, 1998; Michaels, Handfield-Jones & Axelrod, 2001). However, Sparrow (2019) suggests that its historical roots can be traced back several decades before this.

The ascent of talent management as a bona-fide research domain is noteworthy in that it represents a practice and/or consultancy-led phenomenon that took some time before academics started to engage with, seemingly seeing it more as a management fad or fashion (Iles, Preece & Chuai, 2010; Preece, Iles & Chuai, 2011) than a concept which merited scholarly attention. This has seen talent management described as a phenomenon rather than a theory-driven field (Dries, 2013a; Gallardo-Gallardo, Nijs, Dries & Gallo, 2015). It has arguably developed strongly on the back of the appealing and commonly used narrative around the importance of adopting more strategic and systematic approaches to identifying the most value-creating roles within organisations and differentiated approaches to workforce management and HR practices.

This first chapter considers the evolution of talent management as a concept over the past two decades. As such, we briefly discuss the state of the field and how it has evolved over this time. This chapter, therefore, sets the scene for what follows, where we critically review the most dominant and pressing areas of talent management study, along with outlining some of the most pertinent issues facing the field, for its continued development.

Key chapter take-aways

- Talent management remains one of the most critical challenges for organisations and thus continues to be an important research field.
- Talent management has a fragmented body of knowledge but is moving towards greater maturity and coherence.
- More pluralistic perspectives are increasingly entering talent management debates which are to be welcomed as the literature has tended to be overly universalist.
- Talent management should be seen as less about polar extremes in terms of exclusivity versus inclusivity but as more nuanced with workforce differentiation as the central element.
- There is considerable scope to strengthen the research designs underpinning talent management scholarship.

The rise and evolution of talent management

Talent management represents a concept that is both on the rise and in evolution with vibrant debates taking place across academia and practice (Cascio & Aguinis, 2008). It arguably represents one of the fastest-growing domains of management research as evidenced by the explosion of publications, which increasingly find themselves in the top-tier journals (Collings, Scullion & Vaiman, 2015). In a relatively short period of time, the lag in academic research has changed considerably, so much so that Lewis and Heckman's (2006) lament about the lack of scholarly attention no longer stands. Specifically, the past decade has seen an explosion of edited books (Collings, Mellahi & Cascio, 2017; Collings, Scullion & Caligiuri, 2020; Sparrow, Scullion & Tarique, 2014; Vaiman, Schuler, Collings & Sparrow, 2020a, b), review articles (e.g. Lewis & Heckman, 2006; Collings & Mellahi, 2009; McDonnell, Collings, Mellahi & Schuler, 2017; Tarique & Schuler, 2010; Sparrow, 2019; Thunnissen & Gallardo-Gallardo, 2019 – see

Table 1.1.), special journal issues (e.g. Collings, Scullion & Vaiman, 2011; Farndale, Morley & Valverde, 2019; Gallardo-Gallardo, Thunnissen & Scullion, 2020; McDonnell, Collings & Burgess, 2012; Scullion, Collings & Caligiuri, 2010) and journal papers. This publication activity is reinforced by almost ten years of scholarly workshops (i.e. EIASM Talent Management Workshop) and symposia at the leading management conferences such as the annual Academy of Management meeting. All these developments and activities can be viewed as evidence of the development of a burgeoning international community of researchers.

The early years

Talent management has gained a foothold in organisational life because of senior leaders seeing the attraction, development and retention of their top employees as both business-critical and increasingly challenging. The argument put forward by a group of McKinsey consultants in the late 1990s was that shortages of human talent were rapidly emerging across corporate America and that as one of the most valuable organisational resources this was leading to a 'war' for people. Since then, we have witnessed report after report cite talent management as one of the biggest priorities amongst the chief executive and C-suite agendas (e.g. Boston Consulting Group, 2007; Wright, Stewart & Moore, 2011; Erickson, Schwartz & Ensel, 2012; Lanvin & Evans, 2016), and that skills shortages were an omnipresent issue across the developed and emerging world. Globalisation has seen the rise of new and emerging markets, and small to medium-sized enterprises have been on ambitious internationalisation growth paths which has led to increased competition amongst firms for talent, particularly those equipped to work internationally (Tarique & Schuler, 2010). This narrative developed at pace despite the 2008 global economic crisis hitting economies across the world, leading to significant increases in unemployment (McDonnell & Burgess, 2013). It also led to a substantial number of papers focused on talent management in multinational enterprises which saw the emergence of global talent management as an early strand within the literature (McDonnell, Lamare, Gunnigle & Lavelle, 2010; Scullion et al., 2010; Sparrow, Farndale & Scullion, 2013; Stahl et al., 2012).

The earliest period of this nascent field saw most preoccupation with a few issues. Foremost were the many papers talking about definitional and conceptual ambiguity on what talent management meant, with several suggesting that this was slowing the field down from progressing (Lewis & Heckman, 2006; Collings & Mellahi, 2009; Iles, Chuai & Preece, 2010; Tarique & Schuler, 2010). The literature sees highly varied assumptions and limited clarity in respect to defining talent and talent management

(Collings & Mellahi, 2009; Meyers, van Woerkom & Dries, 2013; Dries, 2013b; Wiblen & McDonnell, 2020), with many papers not providing any details on how they were defining the concept (McDonnell et al., 2017). Consequently, the two central concepts were often not defined or saw highly diverse perspectives being taken. In addition, it has only been in more recent times that empirical studies have considered such matters (e.g. Jooss, McDonnell & Burbach, 2019). Moreover, the philosophies underpinning what both talent and talent management concepts mean vary considerably (cf. Collings & Mellahi, 2009; Dries, 2013b; Sparrow & Makram, 2015).

Within these early debates, the extent to which talent management represents an inclusive or exclusive management approach was heavily to the fore (Gallardo-Gallardo, Dries & González-Cruz, 2013; Meyers & van Woerkom, 2014; Swailes, Downs & Orr, 2014; O'Connor & Crowley-Henry, 2019). The dominant view in the literature appears to be that talent management ascribes more to an exclusive type of approach (McDonnell et al., 2017).

We contend that the exclusive versus inclusive debate and commentary have too often been viewed too simplistically and from two extreme positions. The debate often places exclusivity and inclusivity at ends of a continuum – (i.e. everyone should be viewed as talent and treated the same versus one should only focus their attention and investment on a very small percentage of their workforce) – with little consideration of what may lie in-between. Talent management is a more complex concept than this binary dichotomy and inclusivity and exclusivity may exist side by side rather than one versus the other. Our perspective is that talent management is firmly focused on strategic workforce differentiation, which may encompass both identifying and distinguishing positions and people (Huselid, Beatty & Becker, 2005), according to perceived potential contribution to the organisation's competitive advantage and individuals' own skill sets and motivations (see Chapter 2 for a full discussion on talent management definitions and conceptualisations). What this means is that a talent management strategy can be inclusive of all staff, but at a point in time some people and/or roles may be prioritised in terms of extra focus or investment.

This ongoing inclusive versus exclusive debate represents just one of several paradoxes around the meaning of talent and practice of talent management. Some of the other dichotomies that are evident in the literature (see for example, Dries, 2013b) include:

- Talent is innate versus talent can be acquired.
- Talent is rare versus talent is everywhere.
- Talent management is focused on what talent organisations want to keep versus what talent they do not want to lose.

- Individuals need to discover or find their talent versus individuals can develop talent in any area.
- Talent in individuals is stable versus talent is fluid or dynamic.
- Talent as a noun (attributed to what individuals possess) versus talent as a verb (performative construct where individuals perform and show their talent).
- Talent is contextually specific versus talent is transferrable.
- Focus is on potential versus performance or both.

Moving from dichotomisation and universalism to a complex and multilevel phenomena

In more recent years, we see greater appreciation that talent management is a complex concept and that a more multidisciplinary lens may be useful. Notwithstanding criticism on conceptual and theoretical weaknesses, there is evidence that the field is evolving with Sparrow's (2019) fascinating historical analysis of talent management critiques ending with the assertion:

> whilst there is evidence of periodic ideological interpretations of talent management, and grounds for concern over a lack of focus, there has nonetheless been a logical progressive and issues-driven evolution of ideas in the field.
>
> (p. 168)

This positive outlook is encouraging, although there remains a road to be travelled in truly understanding how, when and where talent management is most effective (Sparrow, 2019). We suggest that greater treatment of talent management as a multilevel phenomenon may well be a key enabling mechanism for stronger theory generation. A somewhat unbalanced picture emerges when talent management scholarship is considered from macro-, micro- and meso-level perspectives; in effect it is apparent that the meso-level perspective is dominant (McDonnell et al., 2017).

Macro talent management, which considers the stock of human capital within nation states and the flow of skilled workers across borders, has been markedly absent until recently (see, for example, Khilji, Tarique & Schuler, 2015; King & Vaiman, 2019; Vaiman, Sparrow, Schuler & Collings, 2019a, b). The inclusion of a macro perspective is important because talent management practice will be heavily impacted by factors such as changing demographic profiles, global labour mobility, skills shortages, and increased competition in the marketplace for talent. For example, there appears to be a greater emphasis placed on external hiring and the external labour market in some countries than others which have a more internal labour market focus (Cappelli & Keller, 2014). Moreover, the COVID-19 pandemic offers an especially acute shock that is likely to have a major, if yet unknown, impact on talent management. This effect may be felt across macro, meso and micro levels.

Meso talent management has been the most considered level of analysis (Sparrow, 2019), with organisational-level perspectives involving senior managers as the sole, or primary, participants in common empirical studies (McDonnell et al., 2017). This means the primary focus of research is from the organisational perspective and the talent management practices purported to be in place (see Chapters 4 and 5), alongside the relationship, if any, between these and conceptualisations of talent (Festing, Kornau & Schäfer, 2015; McDonnell et al., 2017). Given the HRM literature which tends to show key differences between intended and actual practices (Sonnenberg, van Zijderveld & Brinks, 2014; Wright & Nishii, 2013), the overwhelming approach of managerial respondents is problematic. Relatively speaking, it is argued that there has been a heavy interest in talent identification and attraction practices and issues (Gallardo-Gallardo & Thunnissen, 2016), with slowly increasing attentiveness to matters of development and retention (Thunnissen & Gallardo-Gallardo, 2019). This meso-level focus is also heavily evident in the global talent management literature (see for example, King, 2015).

The micro level, focusing on the individual or employee perspective, has received considerably less attention (Daubner-Siva, Ybema, Vinkenburg & Beech, 2018; De Boeck, Meyers & Dries, 2018; King, 2016; McDonnell et al., 2017) but, as discussed in Chapter 6, it is an improving situation (Thunnissen & Gallardo-Gallardo, 2019). Emerging research provides some support for positive effects of talent management for individuals (Björkman, Ehrnrooth, Mäkelä, Smale & Sumelius, 2013; Gelens, Dries, Hofmans & Pepermans, 2013). However, the effect size may be less than typically perceived (De Boeck et al., 2018), and a more complex relationship of reciprocity appears to exist (Ehrnrooth et al., 2018).

On the theme of complexity, Wiblen and McDonnell (2020) consider several ways that researchers may consider the operationalisation of talent and talent management meanings, and specific policies and practices at various levels within organisations (see Chapter 3 for a full discussion). There is a recognition that the intersection between differing viewpoints and actions – at the micro, meso and macro levels – could highlight the complexity inherent in evaluating value and resource allocation within organisational boundaries, which tends to be at the heart of talent management. The call is for researchers and practitioners alike to consciously reflect on the operationalisation of talent management definitions, practices and outcomes at multiple levels of analysis. As such there is a need to transition beyond the simplistic perspective of viewing organisations as homogenous entities and places of shared meanings (Salzer-Morling, 1998). This talks to the argument of Thunnissen, Boselie and Fruytier (2013) who suggest that talent management is viewed too rationally and appears somewhat disconnected from the organisational context.

No two talent management strategies, therefore, should ever be the same. Talent management strategies are likely to be best when bespoke, customised and tailored for each unique organisational context. Talent management strategies should be informed by and aligned to organisational strategy. Lewis and Heckman (2006) drew our attention to interrelationships between talent management decisions and strategy by encouraging the deliberate analysis of talent decisions within the context of the organisation's specified "strategic talent direction" (p. 151) and the inherent and salient connection between organisational and talent management strategies. Yet, the literature has not considered strategy, organisational strategy, and talent management strategies in much detail (a notable exception being Tansley & Tietze, 2013). As such, accusations of talent management research being decontextualised may be fair (Gallardo-Gallardo et al., 2020). This, we argue, is both surprising and concerning when considering that the talent management literature tends to lean towards the principle of focusing more resources on the most strategically important value-creating positions.

More critical management scholars have started to deliver some stinging rebukes around the overarching arguments and evidence base of talent management. For example, Dundon and Rafferty's (2018) intentionally provocative article argues that talent management over-individualises the employment relationship, which leads to the dangerous situation of placing an aura around a small number of individuals. They argue that insufficient attention is placed on the wider employment relations system of organisations and the different needs workers have and contributions they make. In sum, the emphasis is too focused on simplistic performative aspects and fails to adequately encompass wider influences and working conditions.

While not of the same school of thought, Pfeffer (2001) raised some related concerns around hyper-individualisation whereby teamwork is undervalued over a small number of employees. The concerns raised by Pfeffer (2001) include that too much of a focus on high-performing individuals may lead to a culture of arrogance and which in turn may inhibit key organisational processes such as knowledge-sharing. Linked to this, we have also witnessed the emergence of a literature that questions the ethicality of talent management. For example, Downs and Swailes (2013) call for a new ethical approach to how talent management is conceptualised and practiced. They raise concerns about the dark side of talent management in bringing harmful individual and organisational outcomes. The concerns once again rest heavily on the overemphasis of the individual, the narrow dimensions taken to measure performance and the lack of wider social and ethical considerations. At the heart of these ethical concerns are the ideals of exclusivity. In the more 'extreme' exclusivity and elitism perspectives, the language that proliferates may be viewed as seeking to exclude employees. This arguably dehumanises people (Haslam, 2006) and the diverse and important contributions they make to workplaces and organisational success.

Language and meaning are therefore very important. These are matters that have not received sufficient empirical investigation and, as such, remain live concerns worthy of scholarly attention. Adopting a more pluralist frame of reference beyond the dominant universalist approach is important in moving our understanding and knowledge forward in what is a far more complex concept than the popular narrative often intimates.

Theory, methods and data: a concise evaluation of the state of the field

There has been much talk around the nature and quality of the conceptualisation and theoretical development of talent management. When one considers the vastness of the research questions that have been considered to date, it is perhaps unsurprising to see some incoherence of theoretical development. By greater unification of the boundaries of the field and the adoption of more multilevel approaches, theoretical advancement will be furthered because it helps ensure that we are talking about similar things. Too often researchers provide insufficient clarity on how they are treating the central concepts and how these are measured (Thunnissen & Gallardo-Gallardo, 2019).

Theoretical frameworks within this specific literature have encompassed the resource-based view, social exchange theory, signalling theory, institutional theory, learning theory and others (McDonnell et al., 2017). More concerning than the variety of theoretical approaches and lack of a grand theory, which we suggest may be a futile pursuit given the diversity of research questions, is that almost half of all published papers did not even mention a theoretical framework (Thunnissen & Gallardo-Gallardo, 2019). In other words, these papers do not use any existing theory nor develop a new theory. Thunnissen and Gallardo-Gallardo (2019) add that where theory is used, it tends to be more superficial in that it is often used to provide justification for introducing a paper rather than a real thorough application of theory to draw out new perspectives. As such the calls that remain for "more fundamental theoretical scaffolding" (Farndale et al., 2019, p. 156) are unsurprising and needed. However, Farndale et al. (2019) also observe that the array of applied and academic perspectives evident in this literature may prove as much a strength as a weakness over time, but this will rest heavily on the "capacity to coalesce dispersed theoretical insights and engage in robust evaluation studies" (p. 155).

In this vein, Sparrow's (2019) analysis is intriguing in suggesting that talent management has been heavily shaped by what he terms six "enabling concepts" (p. 162), all of which are long-standing in the HRM literature. These enabling concepts include the employee life-cycle perspective, competency movement, portfolio thinking, HR planning movement, informated workplaces and the intellectual movement from paying for the job to paying for the person. It may be argued that while many of the ideas taken from such concepts have added greatly to talent management understanding, there has also been perhaps an insufficient critical questioning of all assumptions made which have been central to some of the criticisms levelled at the field. Accordingly, there is scope for more considered theorisation.

The field is made up of more empirical papers than conceptual or theoretical types (McDonnell et al., 2017). However, this is a changed situation compared to previous reviews where empirical work was noted as scarce (e.g. Collings & Mellahi, 2009; Lewis & Heckman, 2006; Thunnissen et al., 2013). We can see from the various review papers that quantitative rather than qualitative studies dominate, with small numbers adopting a mixed methods approach (McDonnell et al., 2017; Thunnissen & Gallardo-Gallardo, 2019). This may in part explain the limitations of theorisation as greater developments will result from more in-depth qualitative designs as the starting point before testing for generalisability. There is a dominance of large, private-sector organisations and especially multinational enterprises with a relative absence of consideration of public-sector and small-to-medium-sized organisations (McDonnell et al., 2017). The emerging empirical base offers encouragement in that we are seeing greater representation of those less-considered stakeholders (e.g. individual employees/talents). The quality of the underlying data on which the field is based has been a source of concern (see Thunnissen & Gallardo-Gallardo, 2019). It is, however, important to acknowledge that more sophisticated approaches are likely to evolve as a field matures, just like in any new research domain (see Chapter 7).

Book structure

The structure of this book is as follows. Chapter 2 considers the definitions, conceptualisations and frameworks that are featured in the extant literature. This chapter demonstrates that talent management is framed in different but somewhat interrelated ways with no clear unified perspective readily apparent. However, as the chapter will show, the literature does display a range of prescriptive and normative assumptions on what effective talent management may look like. The chapter also considers the important debate as to whether talent management and human resource management are in fact distinct. The literature intimates that they are not synonymous, with a key contrast being the differentiation aspect where not all employees are aware of nor partake in talent management practices.

The third chapter recognises that talent is a socially constructed phenomenon. Rather than a normative concept, individuals, teams, units and organisations negotiate what talent is taken to mean within their own context. As a result, talent can mean many things, from every worker being viewed as a talent, to being the gifted few, to those in critical roles, to those who have a specific skill set and so on. Within this chapter, we highlight the four most common ways in which talent is conceptualised. A key argument made is that talent management can be enacted based on multiple different definitions of talent. Given the diversity of perspectives, it is concerning that much of the extant literature fails to set out how they 'treat' or define talent within their study.

In Chapter 4 the focus turns to providing an overview of the different perspectives of how organisations could, should and do identify talent. Following from the preceding chapters, we explore how talent meanings inform and shape talent identification, with the most dominant of meanings embedded within talent management systems and frameworks. We argue that given the centrality of workforce differentiation, it is talent identification which represents the foundational talent management practice. If an organisation seeks to effectively manage its talent, then it has to first identify the 'talent'. The chapter notes that there are key pivot points for talent identification such as the focus on performance versus/or/and the potential aim to be consistent while flexible, and the importance of transparency in making decisions on talent status. It also emphasises how talent determinations are undertaken in terms of systematic, observational and more measurable approaches which are regularly called for, alongside the role of intuition, subjectivity and adhocness.

Chapter 5 turns to the domain of talent development which is a strategic practice that sees investments made towards focused activities that will impact strategy execution. The chapter identifies two ways to frame talent development: 1) developing specific individuals; and 2) developing talent pools. Despite the centrality of development to the notion of effective talent management, the chapter highlights the dearth of empirical studies. This is despite the discourse about the importance of development and investment in talent.

Chapter 6 considers what evidence exists on the purported relationship between talent management and performance at the organisational and individual levels. Within this chapter, we learn that in spite of the often-cited importance of talent management to business success, there is mixed evidence on its impact. While there is a common assumption that talent management leads to positive outcomes for both individuals identified as talent and organisations effectively managing them, the story is more complex than this. An especially important aspect that has received very limited attention to date is the possible negative ramifications that talent status and talent management may have on individuals in receipt of this 'special attention'.

Chapter 7 turns to the future of talent management. Here we return to several elements from earlier chapters to unpack where future research endeavours may be best served. Additionally, we cast the net wider and consider several areas that thus far have been more peripheral aspects of the talent management field but which we believe should be more prominent in research studies over the next decade.

Conclusion

This opening chapter has provided a brief overview of the rise and development of talent management as a field of scholarly enquiry (see Table 1.1 for a summary of useful academic review papers). The key developments over the past two decades are arguably logical and progressive when considered in retrospect (Sparrow, 2019). Debates about definitions and theoretical and conceptual boundaries are important and common aspects of a budding research stream and community. Some of the criticisms around definitional and conceptual ambiguity are arguably no different from most emergent phenomena in the management sciences. While concerns have been expressed that too much consideration has been given to definitional aspects around talent and talent management, this, we argue, remains fundamentally important because this forms the very bedrock of the field. The development of consensus on a field's conceptual parameters should take time as doing so quickly may lead to an overly narrow and constrained view, thus restricting the pursuit of important research agendas.

So where is the field currently? Reading the subsequent chapters will greatly assist readers in determining their own answer to this question. The conclusion from the systematic review undertaken by McDonnell et al. (2017, p. 120) intimated that "a long, windy road" remains to be navigated "before it reaches maturity". They argued that the literature was somewhat fragmented and would benefit from the development of a more common paradigm around the intellectual boundaries of the field, but also that advancement was evident. Some years on from this we would share this perspective. It is a literature that is progressing year on year as a critical mass of research continues to develop. Talent management is a concept that practitioners continue to see as vitally important. As such it represents an area where scholars can have a strong impact and thus reduce the often-cited academia-practice divide.

Table 1.1 Summary of key talent management review papers

Source	Type of review	Key findings
Thunnissen and Gallardo-Gallardo (2019)	Systematic content analysis of 174 refereed articles from 2006 and 2017	Outlines nine key issues impacting the quality of existing talent management research. Calls for improved sophistication in talent management research and greater practitioner/academic collaboration.
Sparrow (2019)	Historical analysis of talent management critiques	Proposes that talent management research has been heavily shaped by what he terms six "enabling concepts". Suggests the field is developing in a solid and logical manner.
De Boeck et al. (2018)	Systematic review of literature focused on employee reactions to talent management	The type of talent management practice is important in how employees react (e.g. employee-centric practices appear most useful). Overall existing evidence indicates some positive affective, behavioural and cognitive effects of talent management, but there may also be negative impacts which have received particularly scant attention.
McDonnell et al. (2017)	Systematic review of talent management scholarship incorporating 88 papers	Identifies two key dominant literature streams, namely the management of high performers/high potentials, and the identification of strategic positions and talent management systems. Suggests that while global talent management is a topic of much attention, much of the published works can be incorporated within those two streams.
Gallardo-Gallardo and Thunnissen (2016)	Systematic review of 96 empirical talent management papers	Suggests a dominance of Anglo-Saxon research but indicates that research designs lack rigour.
Gallardo-Gallardo et al. (2015)	Adopts a bibliometric and content analysis to review the state of the field	Provides a snapshot of publication volume and where papers are published; most cited articles and authors, common methods used.

Source	Type of review	Key findings
Cappelli and Keller (2014)	Reviews conceptual and practical literature on talent management	Concludes that very little is known about more contemporary talent management practices, lacking the most descriptive data of how firms manage challenges. Calls for empirical work that better delineates the strategic jobs concept in practice, with a particular emphasis on non-C-suite roles.
Nijs et al. (2014)	Multidisciplinary review of the definition, operationalisation and measurement of talent	Uses the proposed relationship between talent and performance excellence as an overarching frame; 11 research propositions are set out.
Meyers et al. (2013)	Reviews the meaning of talent from different disciplinary perspectives	Proposes a continuum of the meaning of talent ranging from innate to completely acquired. Argues that the perspective adopted will influence talent management practice.
Tarique and Schuler (2010)	Reviews papers classified as global talent management	Proposes an integrative global talent management (GTM) framework incorporating endogenous and exogenous drivers, GTM system and effectiveness factors.
Collings and Mellahi (2009)	Reviews talent management literature	Proposes a definition of talent management and a strategic talent management model.
Lewis and Heckman (2006)	First review of what talent management is and underlying scientific principles	Notes that there is no clear meaning evident to talent management, with three common perspectives ranging from it being a mere relabeling of HR to a far more distinct and discrete strategic management activity.

References

Björkman, I., Ehrnrooth, M., Mäkelä, K., Smale, A. & Sumelius, J. (2013). Talent or not? Employee reactions to talent identification, *Human Resource Management*, 52: 195–214.

Boston Consulting Group. (2007). *The Future of HR: Key Challenges Through 2015*, Dusseldorf: Boston Consulting Group.

Cappelli, P. & Keller, J. R. (2014). Talent management: Conceptual approaches and practical challenges, *Annual Review of Organizational Psychology and Organizational Behavior*, 1: 305–331.

Cascio, W. F. & Aguinis, H. (2008). Research in industrial and organizational psychology from 1963 to 2007: Changes, choices, and trends, *Journal of Applied Psychology*, 93: 1062–1081.

Chambers, E. G., Foulon, M., Handfield-Jones, H. & Michaels, E. (1998). The war for talent, *McKinsey Quarterly*, 3: 44–57.

Collings, D. G. & Mellahi, K. (2009). Strategic talent management: A review and research agenda, *Human Resource Management Review*, 19: 304–313.

Collings, D. G., Mellahi, K. & Cascio, W. (Eds.). (2017). *The Oxford Handbook of Talent Management*, Oxford: Oxford University Press.

Collings, D. G., Scullion, H. & Vaiman, V. (2011). European perspectives on talent management, *European Journal of International Management*, 5: 454–462.

Collings, D. G., Scullion, H. & Vaiman, V. (2015). Talent management: Progress and prospects, *Human Resource Management Review*, 25: 233–235.

Collings, H., Scullion, D. G. & Caligiuri, P. (Eds.). (2020). *Global Talent Management*, London and New York: Routledge.

Daubner-Siva, D., Ybema, S., Vinkenburg, C. J. & Beech, N. (2018). The talent paradox: Talent management as a mixed blessing, *Journal of Organizational Ethnography*, 7: 74–86.

De Boeck, G., Meyers, M. C. & Dries, N (2018). Employee reactions to talent management: Assumptions versus evidence, *Journal of Organizational Behavior*, 39: 199–213.

Downs, Y. & Swailes, S. (2013). A capability approach to organizational talent management, *Human Resource Development International*, 16: 267–281.

Dries, N. (2013a). Special issue – Talent management, from phenomenon to theory, *Human Resource Management Review*, 23: 267–271.

Dries, N. (2013b). The psychology of talent management: A review and research agenda, *Human Resource Management Review*, 23: 272–285.

Dundon, T. & Rafferty, A. (2018). The (potential) demise of HRM? *Human Resource Management Journal*, 28: 377–391.

Ehrnrooth, M., Björkman, I., Mäkelä, K., Smale, A., Sumelius, J. & Taimitarha, S. (2018). Talent responses to talent status awareness – Not a question of simple reciprocation, *Human Resource Management Journal*, 28: 443–461.

Erickson, R., Schwartz, J. & Ensell, J. (2012). The talent paradox: Critical skills, recession and the illusion of plentitude, *Deloitte Review*, 10: 78–91.

Farndale, E., Morley, M. J. & Valverde, M. (2019). Talent management: Quo vadis? *BRQ Business Research Quarterly*, 22: 155–159.

Festing, M., Kornau, A. & Schäfer, L. (2015). Think talent – Think male? A comparative case study analysis of gender inclusion in talent management practices in the German media industry, *The International Journal of Human Resource Management*, 26: 707–732.

Gallardo-Gallardo, E., Dries, N. & González-Cruz, T. F. (2013). What is the meaning of "talent" in the world of work? *Human Resource Management Review*, 23: 290–300.

Gallardo-Gallardo, E., Nijs, S., Dries, N. & Gallo, P. (2015). Towards an understanding of talent management as a phenomenon-driven field using bibliometric and content analysis, *Human Resource Management Review*, 25: 264–279.

Gallardo-Gallardo, E. & Thunnissen, M. (2016). Standing on the shoulders of giants? A critical review of empirical talent management research, *Employee Relations*, 38: 31–56.

Gallardo-Gallardo, E., Thunnissen, M. & Scullion, H. (2020). Talent management: Context matters, *The International Journal of Human Resource Management*, 31: 457–473.

Gelens, J., Dries, N., Hofmans, J., Pepermans, R. (2013). The role of perceived organizational justice in shaping the outcomes of talent management: A research agenda, *Human Resource Management Review*, 23: 341–353.

Haslam, N. (2006). Dehumanization: An integrative review, *Personality and Social Psychology Review*, 10: 253–265.

Huselid, M. A., Beatty, R. W. & Becker, B. E. (2005). "A players" or "A positions"? The strategic logic of workforce management, *Harvard Business Review*, December, 110–117.

Iles, P., Chuai, X. & Preece, D. (2010). Talent management and HRM in multinational companies in Beijing: Definitions, differences and drivers, *Journal of World Business*, 45: 179–189.

Iles, P., Preece, D. & Chuai, X. (2010). Talent management as a management fashion in HRD: Towards a research agenda, *Human Resource Development International*, 13: 125–145.

Jooss, S., McDonnell, A. & Burbach, R. (2019). Talent designation in practice. An equation of high potential, performance and mobility, *The International Journal of Human Resource Management*. https://doi.org/10.1080/09585192.2019.1686651

Khilji, S. E., Tarique, I. & Schuler, R. (2015). Incorporating the macro view in global talent management, *Human Resource Management Review*, 25: 236–248.

King, K. A. (2015). Global talent management. Introducing a strategic framework and multiple-actors model, *Journal of Global Mobility*, 3: 273–288.

King, K. A. (2016). The talent deal and journey: Understanding how employees respond to talent identification over time, *Employee Relations*, 38(1): 94–111.

King, K. A. & Vaiman, V. (2019). Enabling effective talent management through a macro-contingent approach: A framework for research and practice, *BRQ Business Research Quarterly*, 22: 194–206.

Lanvin, B. & Evans, P. (2016). *The Global Competitiveness Index 2017: Talent and Technology*, Fontainebleau, France: INSEAD, Adecco & HCLI.

Lewis, R. E. & Heckman, R. J. (2006). Talent management: A critical review, *Human Resource Management Review*, 16: 139–154.

McDonnell, A. & Burgess, J. (2013). The impact of the global financial crisis on managing employees, *International Journal of Manpower*, 34: 184–197.

McDonnell, A., Collings, D. G. & Burgess, J. (2012). Talent management in the Asia-Pacific, *Asia Pacific Journal of Human Resources*, 50: 391–398.

McDonnell, A., Collings, D. G., Mellahi, K. & Schuler, R. S. (2017). Talent management: A systematic review and future research agenda, *European Journal of International Management*, 11: 86–128.

McDonnell, A., Lamare, R., Gunnigle, P. & Lavelle, J. (2010). Developing tomorrow's leaders – Evidence of global talent management in multinational enterprises, *Journal of World Business*, 45: 150–160.

Meyers, M. C. & van Woerkom, M. (2014). The influence of underlying philosophies on talent management: Theory, implications for practice, and research agenda, *Journal of World Business*, 49: 192–203.

Meyers, M. C., van Woerkom, M. & Dries, N. (2013). Talent – Innate or acquired? Theoretical considerations and their implications for talent management, *Human Resource Management Review*, 23: 305–321.

Michaels, E., Handfield-Jones, H. & Axelrod, B. (2001). *The War for Talent*, Boston: Harvard Business School.

Nijs, S., Gallardo-Gallardo, E., Dries, N. & Sels, L. (2014). A multidisciplinary review into the definition, operationalization, and measurement of talent, *Journal of World Business*, 49: 180–191.

O'Connor, E. & Crowley-Henry, M. (2019). Exploring the relationship between exclusive talent management, perceived organizational justice and employee engagement: Bridging the literature, *Journal of Business Ethics*, 156: 903–917.

Pfeffer, J. (2001). Fighting the war for talent is hazardous to your organization's health, *Organizational Dynamics*, 29: 248–259.

Preece, D., Iles, P. & Chuai, X. (2011). Talent management and management fashion in Chinese enterprises: Exploring case studies in Beijing, *The International Journal of Human Resource Management*, 22: 3413–3428.

Salzer-Morling, M. (1998). As God created the Earth. . . A saga that makes sense?, in D. Grant, T. Keenoy & C. Oswick (Eds.), *Discourse and Organizationm*, London, UK: Sage, pp. 104–118.

Scullion, H., Collings, D. G. & Caligiuri, P. (2010). Global talent management, *Journal of World Business*, 45: 105–108.

Sonnenberg, M., van Zijderveld, V. & Brinks, M. (2014). The role of talent-perception incongruence in effective talent management, *Journal of World Business*, 49: 272–280.

Sparrow, P. R. (2019). A historical analysis of critiques in the talent management debate, *BRQ Business Research Quarterly*, 22: 160–170.

Sparrow, P. R., Farndale, E. & Scullion, H. (2013). An empirical study of the role of the corporate HR function in global talent management in professional and financial service firms in the global financial crisis, *The International Journal of Human Resource Management*, 24: 1777–1798.

Sparrow, P. R. & Makram, H. (2015). What is the value of talent management? Building value-driven processes within a talent management architecture, *Human Resource Management Review*, 25: 249–263.

Sparrow, P. R., Scullion, H. & Tarique, I. (Eds.). (2014). *Strategic Talent Management: Contemporary Issues in International Context*, Cambridge: Cambridge University Press.

Stahl, G., Björkman, I., Farndale, E., Morris, S. S., Paauwe, J., Stiles, P., Trevor, J. & Wright, P. (2012). Six principles of effective global talent management, *Sloan Management Review*, 53: 25–42.

Swailes, S., Downs, Y. & Orr, K. (2014). Conceptualising inclusive talent management: Potential, possibilities and practicalities, *Human Resource Development International*, 17: 529–544.

Tansley, C. & Tietze, S. (2013). Rites of passage through talent management progression stages: An identity work perspective, *The International Journal of Human Resource Management*, 24: 1799–1815.

Tarique, I. & Schuler, R. S. (2010). Global talent management: Literature review, integrative framework, and suggestions for further research, *Journal of World Business*, 45: 122–133.

Thunnissen, M., Boselie, P. & Fruytier, B. (2013). A review of talent management: "Infancy or adolescence"? *International Journal of Human Resource Management*, 24: 1744–1761.

Thunnissen, M. & Gallardo-Gallardo, E. (2019). Rigor and relevance in empirical TM research: Key issues and challenges, *BRQ Business Research Quarterly*, 22: 171–180.

Vaiman, V., Schuler, R. S., Collings, D. G. & Sparrow, P. (Eds.). (2020a). *Macro Talent Management in Emerging and Emergent Markets*, London and New York: Routledge.

Vaiman, V., Schuler, R. S., Collings, D. G. & Sparrow, P. (Eds.). (2020b). *Macro Talent Management: A Global Perspective on Managing Talent in Developed Markets*, London and New York: Routledge.

Vaiman, V., Sparrow, P., Schuler, R. S. & Collings, D. G. (Eds.). (2020a). *Macro Talent Management in Emerging and Emergent Markets*, London and New York: Routledge.

Vaiman, V., Sparrow, P., Schuler, R. S. & Collings, D. G. (Eds.). (2020b). *Macro Talent Management: A Global Perspective on Managing Talent in Developed Markets*, London and New York: Routledge.

Wiblen, S. & McDonnell, A. (2020). Connecting talent meanings and multi-level context: A discursive approach, *The International Journal of Human Resource Management*, 31: 474–510.

Wright, P. M. & Nishii, L. (2013). Strategic HRM and organizational behaviour: Integrating multiple levels of analysis, in J. Paauwe, D. Guest & P. Wright (Eds.), *HRM and Performance: Achievements and Challenges*, Chichester: Wiley, pp. 97–110.

Wright, P. M., Stewart, M. & Moore, A. (2011). *The 2011 CHRO Challenge: Building Organizational, Functional, and Personal Talent*, Ithaca, NY: Cornell.

2 'Talent management' definitions, conceptualisations and frameworks

Introduction

Research within Strategic Human Resource Management (SHRM) and talent management is undoubtedly subject to contested terrain as various texts, especially earlier publications, focused on establishing (arbitrary) boundaries between the two (Iles, Chuai & Preece, 2010; Lewis & Heckman, 2006). While we concede that there is a need within academia to distinguish between different research domains, we do not seek to reconcile these approaches here in this book. We require a more informed understanding of talent and the talent management phenomena as the two terms are omnipresent in the corporate lexicon. There is a danger of researchers getting too enshrined in debates on somewhat semantic and definitional differences which are unhelpful in moving knowledge forward and providing for more informed and effective practice. Definitional consensus is something we suggest is not especially common across many management concepts, rather than being a unique feature of talent management. Engaging in definitional debates may distract researchers from more thorough and important matters about individual, interpersonal and organisational talent management meanings and practices and examining the tensions organisations face when organising and mobilising workforces for strategy execution, financial gains and employee wellness.

This chapter provides an overview of the various perspectives of talent management including consideration of the definitions, conceptualisations and frameworks featuring in existing publications. Given the variation, the chapter highlights dominant and parallel understandings. While highlighting the absence of a unified perspective and frame, the chapter will show that there are several normative and prescriptive assumptions about the basis and focus of effective talent management. Specifically, the chapter depicts the literature as conceptualising talent management in five ways:

1 talent management as the same thing as HRM.
2 the creation of talent pools.

3 the management of designated individuals.
4 a set of practices with a focus on pivotal roles.
5 a set of judgment-based decisions.

The chapter highlights that while HRM focuses on the policies and practices which apply to everyone; talent management focuses on differentiation and segmentation with policies, practices and resource allocation enacted upon the importance of positions and persons, meaning 'some' may receive disproportionate attention. Academics past, present and future can build upon some or all of these, given these perspectives offer a legitimate way to understand and examine talent management phenomena.

Key chapter take-aways

• Academics frame talent management in different, but interrelated, ways with numerous definitions, conceptualisations and frameworks presented in existing publications.
• HRM and talent management are not synonymous because talent management emphasises that 'some' individuals or talent pools are privy to talent management practices, while others are not.

Talent management definitions

To date, there has been little agreement on what talent management 'is', with academics proposing various definitions which in turn have guided and shaped how it has been examined in research. One major issue associated with offering suggestions of how organisations could and should define and conceptualise talent management are questions about 'who' – which individuals or groups of individuals – and 'what' – the policies and practices – are associated with managing talent.

Reflective consideration of the evolution of talent management and the definitions presented in Table 2.1 illustrate the diverse perspectives, as well as the emphasis on 'some' rather than 'all' of an organisation's workforce, which dominate the literature. Regardless of academic views, it is imperative that researchers specifically ask about what the term talent management means and how various organisational stakeholders think about and frame talent management within the context of their everyday activities, interactions and strategic operations, given meanings may differ even if similar terms are used (Wiblen & McDonnell, 2020). Perhaps more problematic is that while organisations often depict themselves as allocating considerable time and resources towards talent management, they often do this without a working definition of what talent management means to them in their organisational context (CIPD, 2006a, b; Boston Consulting Group, 2007).

Table 2.1 Examples of talent management definitions and conceptualisations

Definitions and conceptualisations	Source	Talent management as ...	The 'what' The 'something'	The 'who' The 'someone'
Talent management should be proactive and be based on the identification, selection and nurturing of key performers, the sourcing, development and allocation of replacements for key personnel and the allocation of resources to key talent; contingent on their value to the firm.	Berger and Berger (2003)	Management of designated individuals A set of practices	Identification Selection Nurturing Allocation of resources	Individuals (performers)
Talent management includes sourcing, screening, selection, retention, development and renewal of the workforce with analysis and planning.	Schweyer (2004)	Similar to HRM Creation of talent pools	Sourcing Screening Selection Workforce planning Development Retention	Individuals (everyone)
The practice of talent management involves a number of specific processes including workforce planning, talent gap analysis, recruiting, staffing, education, development, retention, talent reviews, succession planning and evaluation.	McCauley and Wakefield (2006)	Similar to HRM Creation of talent pools	Workforce planning Gap analysis Recruiting Staffing Education Development Retention Reviews Succession planning Evaluation	Individuals (everyone)
Talent management refers to the additional management, processes and opportunities that are made available to people in the organisation who are considered talent.	Blass (2007, p. 3)	Management of designated individuals	Additional opportunities	Individuals (talent)

Definition	Source		Activities	Focus
The talent management programme features a strong emphasis on "high potentials", so our conception of talent management specifically involves attracting, selecting, developing and retaining high-potential employees.	Stahl et al. (2007, pp. 4–5)	Set of practices Management of designated individuals	Attraction Selection Development Retention	Individuals (potential)
Talent management can be defined as the strategic integrated approach to managing a career from attracting, retaining and developing to transitioning the organisation's human resources.	van Dijk (2008, p. 385)	Similar to HRM Management of designated individuals	Attraction Development Retention	Individuals (everyone)
Talent management is a comprehensive set of processes designed to manage a company's greatest asset: people.	Snell (2008)	Similar to HRM		Individuals (everyone)
Activities and processes that involve the systematic identification of key positions which differentially contribute to the organisation's sustainable competitive advantage, the development of a talent pool of high-potential and high-performing incumbents to fill these roles and the development of a differentiated human resource architecture to facilitate the filling of these positions with competent incumbents and to ensure their continued commitment to the organisation.	Collings and Mellahi (2009, p. 304)	A set of practices Creation of talent pools	Identification Development	Positions Individuals – groups of designated individuals (performance and potential)
Talent management typically focuses on a specified pool of employees who rank at the top in terms of capability and performance.	Mäkelä, Björkman and Ehrnrooth (2010, p. 135)	Creation of talent pools Management of designated individuals	Attraction Development Retention	Individuals – a group of individuals (capability/ performance)
Talent management refers to an organisation's efforts to attract, develop and retain talented key employees.		A set of practices		Individuals (key)

(Continued)

Table 2.1 (Continued)

Definitions and conceptualisations	Source	Talent management as . . .	The 'what' The 'something'	The 'who' The 'someone'
Talent management typically involves the identification, development, appraisal, deployment and retention of high-performing employees. It is a distinct business activity because it calls for greater focus on employees and positions that have the greatest differential impact on business strategy.	McDonnell (2011, p. 169)	A set of practices	Identification Development Appraisal Deployment Retention	Individuals (performance) Positions
Talent management is concerned with developing strategy, identifying talent gaps, succession planning and recruiting, selecting, educating, motivating and retaining talented employees through a variety of initiatives.	Whelan and Carcary (2011, p. 676)	A set of practices	Develop strategy Identify talent gaps Succession planning Recruiting Educating Motivating Retaining	Individuals (talented)
Talent management isn't simply about hiring the best. It's about managing talent appropriately through selection, recruitment, development and rewards.	Aghina, de Jong and Simon (2011, p. 3)	Similar to HRM Management of designated individuals	Selection Recruitment Development Rewards	Individuals (everyone)
Talent management is aimed at the systematic attraction, identification, development, engagement/retention and deployment of high-potential and high-performing employees to fill in key positions which have significant influence on the organisation's sustainable competitive advantage.	Gallardo-Gallardo and Thunnissen (2016, p. 50)	A set of practices Management of designated individuals	Attraction Identification Development Engagement Retention Deployment	Individuals (performance and potential)

Source: Adapted from Wiblen (2015)

This has carried into the publishing world with Thunnissen and Gallardo-Gallardo (2019) highlighting a substantial minority of papers not presenting any clarity on what the authors understood by talent management, and many more providing very vague indications.

Talent management conceptualisations and frameworks

The past two decades have seen a significant increase in the proliferation of conceptual frameworks and categories. Lewis and Heckman (2006) presented the first foundational, yet highly critical, review of talent management. Consideration of the explicit and implicit rhetoric, research and reality of talent management, the authors addressed the question of whether the study of talent management represented separate and discrete phenomena of research from that of SHRM and HRM. In examining both bodies of literature, Lewis and Heckman proposed three distinct perspectives premising talent management as:

1   A collection of HR practices.
2   A set of practices that focus on talent pools.
3   Practices which focus on the management of people-based resources.

Multiple conceptual frameworks, many of which build on Lewis and Heckman's work, have been offered since (for example, see Collings & Mellahi, 2009; Hartmann, Feisel & Schober, 2010; Iles, Chuai et al., 2010; Jones, Whitaker, Seet & Parkin, 2012; Scullion, Collings & Caligiuri, 2010). The most noteworthy in this regard in terms of the traction gained in the wider literature is the paper by Collings and Mellahi (2009). Rather than seek to reconcile debates about the merits of each, we offer a brief overview of several frameworks because each is worthy of consideration as it shapes and influences how we talk and write about talent management today.

Talent management as – like human resource management

The first perspective frames talent management as like HRM with the former representative of a "collection of typical HRM practices, functions or activities" (Lewis & Heckman, 2006, p. 140). From this perspective, talent management aligns with SHRM and may merely involve the rebranding of traditional HRM. Although these practices focus on the management of talent through conventional processes, they are different because they do so in a timelier manner. Talent is equated with human capital (Thunnissen, Boselie & Fruytier, 2013) whereby all employees possess valuable ability and expertise. References to talent are akin to human capital with the two terms applied interchangeably.

Advocates of this stream (see Lewis & Heckman, 2006 for references to these) are commended for possessing a broad view. They are, however, simultaneously criticised because most talent management advocates proactively emphasise that it encompasses more than just traditional HR practices such as recruitment, leadership development and succession planning (Collings & Mellahi, 2009). Talent management differs because it is future-oriented, with practices aligned with strategic goals (Lewis & Heckman, 2006; Schweyer, 2004). This foundational perspective is like SHRM, and on this basis, many concede that talent management may merely represent the relabeling of traditional HRM practices (Collings & Mellahi, 2009). As a result, there has been some reference to Abrahamson's (1996) perspectives around fads and fashions (Iles, Preece & Chuai, 2010). While this is a perspective expressed in the literature, it has received little attention and credence.

Talent management as – the creation of talent pools

The second perspective focuses on resource allocation and attention to the creation of talent pools. This perspective views all employees as valuable resources regardless of the specific needs or strategic aims of an organisation; focuses on establishing a set of processes designed to ensure an adequate flow of employees into jobs throughout the organisation (Lewis & Heckman, 2006). As such it draws heavily on succession planning and manpower planning (Mellahi & Collings, 2010) and is driven by the desire to manage talent pools in relation to specific, mainly senior management and leadership positions (Thunnissen et al., 2013). This perspective would however appear to be a more dynamic approach to succession planning where the focus is on greater consideration of the future value of human capital to various positions, though these roles may not be explicitly mapped out (Lepak, Takeuchi & Swart, 2011). This perspective suggests a more dynamic approach is needed where an organisation has multiple (pools) of people who possess vital base abilities, competencies and knowledge that could with appropriate support and training and development move into one of several roles. This perspective has seen calls for HR to give greater consideration to the use of scenario planning and supply chain management (Cappelli, 2008; Schuler, Jackson & Tarique, 2011). A key criticism here is that it neglects that organisations may possess key talent pools by virtue of particular skills or knowledge they possess that stand outside managerial roles (McDonnell, Gunnigle, Lavelle & Lamare, 2016).

Talent management as – the management of designated individuals

The third stream focuses on the management of talented people (Mellahi & Collings, 2010) without regard for specific positions or organisational boundaries. Lewis and Heckman (2006) propose two views of talent within this approach. The first positions talent concerning high-performing and high-potential employees, where a workforce is divided and managed according to these relative levels. Talent management ordinarily commences with identifying and mobilising internal talent pools (Boudreau & Ramstad, 2005; Bryan, Joyce & Weiss, 2006). Differentiation, according to performance-based criteria and evaluations, enables organisations to fill all roles and positions with 'A Performers'. Organisations also manage lower performers, known as 'C Performers', out of the organisation (Collings & Mellahi, 2009; Michaels, Handfield-Jones & Axelrod, 2001). This approach has seen much discussion and many comments with links to forced distribution or top grading systems as popularised by Jack Welch at GE. The focus is firmly on attracting, retaining and appropriately rewarding the top performers regardless of role (Lewis & Heckman, 2006).

The second view claims that talent is an undifferentiated resource which resides in everyone (an inclusive approach), whereby all individuals have specific abilities and expertise (Thunnissen et al., 2013). The goal of talent management, therefore, is to manage all individuals to their levels of high performance. Thus, the focus is on assisting each employee to reach their own performance capability and peak. Thunnissen et al. (2013) argue, however, that framing talent management as the management of designated individuals, whether from the perspective of pools of high performers or each individual to their high performance, limits our understandings. This is because it ultimately means there is an unhealthy concentration on a single aspect of talent management rather than a more nuanced understanding of what we contend is a complex, multilevel phenomenon.

Talent management as – a set of practices focused on pivotal positions

In recent years there has been an increasing propensity to frame talent management as a set of specific practices. The emphasis attributed to practices per se may stem from attempts to meaningfully differentiate between talent management, SHRM and HRM. Purported talent management 'practices' include talent acquisition (as opposed to recruitment and selection), talent identification (as opposed to performance management) (see Chapter 4), talent development (as opposed to learning and skills development) (see Chapter 5) and retention of those most valuable individuals rather than all staff.

Table 2.1 illustrates the proliferation of talent management as a set of practices and conceptualisations.

Although maintaining a focus on high performance and potential, the talent management as a set of practices approach draws specific attention to the core proposition of workforce differentiation whereby parts of a workforce are privy to these. Other non- or less-talented individuals do not partake in, or are in receipt of, the same practices as their talented counterparts. This perspective also extends previous frameworks by advocating for systematic approaches. Transitioning to systematic approaches seeks to overcome the potential negative implications and effects of ad hoc practices (see Chapter 4 for an extensive discussion). A systematic set of talent-based practices also builds on the notion of a talent-based science promoted by John Boudreau and Peter Ramstad (see Boudreau & Ramstad, 2005, 2006, 2007). Moreover, the HR architecture literature (e.g. Lepak & Snell, 1999, 2002) is regularly mentioned in this regard (Collings & Mellahi, 2009; McDonnell, Lamare, Gunnigle & Lavelle, 2010).

The Collings and Mellahi (2009) perspective is perhaps the most accepted approach in the literature (Claussen, Grohsjean, Luger & Probst, 2014; Gallardo-Gallardo, Nijs, Dries & Gallo, 2015 Jones et al., 2012; Sidani & Al Ariss, 2014). This articulation of focusing on key positions along with talent management practices is noteworthy in that it recognises that these can and are likely to encompass roles outside the top management team. Key positions, for example, could reside at organisational levels beyond the top management team, those that have a differential impact on the organisation's competitive advantage (McDonnell et al., 2016). Moreover, the argument is that it is the identification of pivotal roles which represents the starting point as opposed to commencing with a people focus. Critical roles represent those that have a disproportionate impact on an organisation's strategic objectives and where the variability of performance in the role substantially impacts, positively or negatively, the organisation's ability to execute its strategy (Huselid, Beatty & Becker, 2005). In this vein, Boudreau and Ramstad (2007) call on organisations to assess where changes in talent will have the highest impact on strategy execution. It is argued that once a performance threshold has been reached in some positions, that is sufficient. In other words, significantly improved value may not result from higher performance in such a role. Consequently, this is a key difference in pivotal versus important roles.

> [we] define strategic talent management as activities and processes that involve the systematic identification of key positions which differentially contribute to an organisation's sustainable competitive advantage, the development of a talent pool of high potential and high performing

incumbents to fill these roles, and the development of a differentiated human resource architecture to facilitate filling these positions with the best available incumbent and to ensure their continued commitment to the organisation.

(Collings & Mellahi, 2009, p. 304)

This perspective advocates a top-down approach in that it does not assume all roles need to be filled by 'A' players. What, however, is vital is ensuring that the 'best' people fill those pivotal positions to help realise appropriate organisational (e.g. economic) value (Boxall & Purcell, 2011). As such this perspective implicitly sets out the importance of an organisation's strategy (McDonnell, 2011), something ill-considered in much of the research (Wiblen & McDonnell, 2020). In the process of campaigning for the mobilisation of specific individuals into key positions, the authors assert that the identification, development and fostering the commitment of high-performing and high-potential talent pools are included in talent management practice.

A key challenge in this stream of literature rests on how organisations can systematise the identification of key positions and the filling of these with appropriate incumbents. We, however, know very little about the extent to which this occurs in practice. In terms of those notable exceptions, the finding is that talent management practices tend to often be ad hoc rather than integrated, systematic or strategic (Hartmann et al., 2010; McDonnell et al., 2010). Similarly, studies by Blass (2007) and Burbach and Royle (2010), while now dated, evidenced a significant disconnect between the rhetoric and realities of managing talent through formalised and intentionally designed practices. Even less frequently, if at all, do they examine whether and how organisations structure and then optimise talent-based systems as per Lewis and Heckman's (2006) observation.

Talent management as – a set of judgment-based decisions

A further way to understand and appreciate what talent management 'is', is to consider the activities required of actors to realise the promoted (beneficial) outcomes. Wiblen (2019, p. 154) suggests that talent management is:

A judgment-orientated activity, where humans make judgments about [the value of] other humans. These judgments, while mediated by various contextual factors and variables (such as technology), should be informed by and aligned to, current and future strategic ambitions and goals.

A judgment-based definition recognises that actors within organisations use talent management – whether talent identification, talent development or talent retention – as a mechanism to decide which individuals receive talent management practices. Talent management, in this vein, includes three main attributes: (1) judgments about value; (2) decisions; and (3) resources. Actors make judgments about the value of individuals within their workforces; relevant stakeholders then make decisions based on judgments of value; decisions about resource allocations are based on prior judgments of value. Talent management sees specifically designated higher-value individuals, known as talent subjects, afforded additional resources (e.g. development opportunities, secondments) than their (perceived) lower-value workforce counterparts. Notably, higher-value individuals gain the time and attention of their respective managers and potentially direct access to the senior leadership team.

Conclusion

This chapter has reported that there are several ideas about how researchers can define and understand talent management. Researchers and practitioners alike are encouraged to appreciate the different definitions, conceptualisations and frameworks operating within existing publications because they are not mutually exclusive. It is important that the approach adopted is articulated, which has tended to be somewhat mixed in existing publications. We suggest that regardless of personal perspectives or preferred frameworks, researchers must acknowledge that workforce differentiation is at the core of talent management. Advocates of talent management agree, from a foundational perspective, that part of the workforce is of higher value (in terms of contributing to the organisation's strategic objectives) because of evaluated performance and/or potential.

Rather than seek to reconcile debates which reside solely in the theoretical domain, researchers and the larger talent management community may benefit from focusing efforts on learning more about how talent management meanings and practices are framed within and by organisations. Understanding talent management at the micro, meso and macro levels is key because what talent management 'is' will be contextually specific. Each organisation must decide 'who' and 'what' talent is and how to identify, mobilise, develop and manage talent subjects via a set of practices within the context of their strategic ambitions and goals.

References

Abrahamson, E. (1996). Management fashion, *Academy of Management Review*, 21: 254–285.
Aghina, W., de Jong, M. & Simon, D. (2011). How the best labs manage talent, *McKinsey Quarterly*, May.

Berger, L. & Berger, D. (Eds.). (2003). *The Talent Management Handbook: Creating a Sustainable Competitive Advantage by Selecting, Developing and Promoting the Best People*, New York: McGraw-Hill Professional.

Blass, E. (2007). *Talent Management: Maximising Talent for Business Performance. Executive Summary November 2007*. Retrieved from London: www.ashridge.org. uk/Website/IC.nsf/wFARPUB/Talent+Management:+Maximising+talent+for+b usiness+performance?opendocument

Boston Consulting Group. (2007). *The Future of HR: Key Challenges Through 2015*, Dusseldorf: Boston Consulting Group.

Boudreau, J. W. & Ramstad, P. M. (2005). Talentship and the new paradigm for human resource management: From professional practices to strategic talent decision science, *Human Resource Planning*, 28: 17–26.

Boudreau, J. W. & Ramstad, P. M. (2006). Talentship and HR measurement and analysis: From ROI to strategic organizational change, *Human Resource Planning*, 29: 25–33.

Boudreau, J. W. & Ramstad, P. M. (2007). *Beyond HR: The New Science of Human Capital*, Boston, MA: Harvard Business School Press.

Bryan, L., Joyce, C. & Weiss, L. (2006). Making a market in talent, *McKinsey Quarterly*, 2: 98–109.

Boxall, P. & Purcell, J. (2011). *Strategy and Human Resource Management*, third edition, Basingsoke: Palgrave Macmillan.

Burbach, R. & Royle, T. (2010). Talent on demand?: Talent management in the German and Irish subsidiaries of a US multinational corporation, *Personnel Review*, 39(4): 414–431.

Cappelli, P. (2008). Talent management for the twenty-first century. *Harvard Business Review*, March, pp. 74–81.

CIPD. (2006a). *Reflections on Talent Management*, London: CIPD.

CIPD. (2006b). *Learning and Development: Annual Survey Report 2006*, London: CIPD.

Claussen, J., Grohsjean, T., Luger, J. & Probst, G. (2014). Talent management and career development: What it takes to get promoted, *Journal of World Business*, 49: 236–244.

Collings, D. G. & Mellahi, K. (2009). Strategic talent management: A review and research agenda, *Human Resource Management Review*, 19: 304–313.

Gallardo-Gallardo, E., Nijs, S., Dries, N. & Gallo, P. (2015). Towards an understanding of talent management as a phenomenon-driven field using bibliometric and content analysis, *Human Resource Management Review*, 25: 264–279.

Gallardo-Gallardo, E. & Thunnissen, M. (2016). Standing on the shoulders of giants? A critical review of empirical talent management research, *Employee Relations*, 38: 31–56.

Hartmann, E., Feisel, E. & Schober, H. (2010). Talent management of western MNCs in China: Balancing global integration and local responsiveness, *Journal of World Business*, 45:169–178.

Huselid, M. A., Beatty, R. W. & Becker, B. E. (2005). "A players" or "A positions"? The strategic logic of workforce management, *Harvard Business Review*, December: 110–117.

Iles, P., Chuai, X. & Preece, D. (2010). Talent management and HRM in multinational companies in Beijing: Definitions, differences and drivers, *Journal of World Business*, 45: 179–189.

Iles, P., Preece, D. & Chuai, X. (2010). Talent management as a management fashion in HRD: Towards a research agenda, *Human Resource Development International*, 13: 125–145.

Jones, J. T., Whitaker, M., Seet, P.-S. & Parkin, J. (2012). Talent management in practice in Australia: Individualistic or strategic? An exploratory study, *Asia Pacific Journal of Human Resources*, 50: 399–420.

Lepak, D. P. & Snell, S. A. (1999). The human resource architecture: Toward a theory of human capital allocation and development, *Academy of Management Review*, 24: 31–48.

Lepak, D. P. & Snell, S. A. (2002). Examining the human resource architecture: The relationships among human capital, employment, and human resource configurations, *Journal of Management*, 28: 517–543.

Lepak, D. P., Takeuchi, R. & Swart, J. (Eds.). (2011). *Aligning Human Capital with Organizational Needs*. Oxford: Oxford University Press.

Lewis, R. E. & Heckman, R. J. (2006). Talent management: A critical review, *Human Resource Management Review*, 16: 139–154.

Mäkelä, K., Björkman, I. & Ehrnrooth, M. (2010). How do MNCs establish their talent pools? Influences on individuals' likelihood of being labelled as talent, *Journal of World Business*, 45: 134–142.

McCauley, C. & Wakefield, M. (2006). Talent management in the 21st century: Help your company find, develop, and keep its strongest workers, *Journal for Quality & Participation*, 29: 4–7.

McDonnell, A. (2011). Still fighting the war for talent? Bridging the science versus practice gap, *Journal of Business and Psychology*, 26: 169–173.

McDonnell, A., Gunnigle, P., Lavelle, J. & Lamare, R. (2016). Beyond managerial and leadership elites: "Key group" identification and differential reward architectures in multinational companies, *The International Journal of Human Resource Management*, 27: 1299–1318.

McDonnell, A., Lamare, R., Gunnigle, P. & Lavelle, J. (2010). Developing tomorrow's leaders- evidence of global talent management in multinational companies, *Journal of World Business*, 45: 150–160.

Mellahi, K. & Collings, D. G. (2010). The barriers to effective global talent management: The example of corporate élites in MNEs, *Journal of World Business*, 45: 143–149.

Michaels, E., Handfield-Jones, H. & Axelrod, B. (2001). *The War for Talent*, Boston: Harvard Business School Press.

Schuler, R. S., Jackson, S.E. & Tarique, I. (2011). Frameworks for global talent management: HR actions for dealing with global talent challenges, in D.G. Collings & H. Scullion (Eds.), *Global Talent Management*, New York: Routledge, pp. 17–36.

Schweyer, A. (2004). *Talent Management Systems: Best Practices in Technology Solutions for Recruitment, Retention and Workforce Planning*, New Jersey: John Wiley and Sons.

Scullion, H., Collings, D. G. & Caligiuri, P. (2010). Global talent management, *Journal of World Business*, 45: 105–108.

Sidani, Y. & Al Ariss, A. (2014). Institutional and corporate drivers of global talent management: Evidence from the Arab Gulf region, *Journal of World Business*, 49: 215–224.

Snell, A. (2008). The future of talent management, *Workforce Management*, 87(20).

Stahl, G., Björkman, I., Farndale, E., Morris, S. S., Paauwe, J., Stiles, P. & Wright, P. M. (2007). Global talent management: How leading multinationals build and sustain their talent pipeline, *INSEAD Working Papers Collection*, 34: 1–36.

Thunnissen, M., Boselie, P. & Fruytier, B. (2013). A review of talent management: "Infancy or adolescence?", *The International Journal of Human Resource Management*, 24: 1744–1761.

Thunnissen, M. & Gallardo-Gallardo, E. (2019). Rigor and relevance in empirical TM research: Key issues and challenges, *BRQ Business Research Quarterly*, 22: 171–180.

Van Dijk, H. G. (2008). The talent management approach to human resource management: Attracting and retaining the right people, *Journal of Public Administration*, 43: 385–395.

Whelan, E. & Carcary, M. (2011). Integrating talent and knowledge management: Where are the benefits? *Journal of Knowledge Management*, 15: 675–687.

Wiblen, S. (2015). *Talking About Talent: Conceptualising Talent Management Through Discourse* (Doctor of Philosophy Ph.D.), University of Sydney Business School Discipline of Work and Organisational Studies. Retrieved from: http://hdl.handle.net/2123/13257

Wiblen, S. (2019). e-Talent in talent management, in M. Thite (Ed.), *e-HRM: Digital Approaches, Directions and Applications*, Milton Park: Routledge, pp. 153–171.

Wiblen, S. & McDonnell, A. (2020). Connecting talent meanings and multi-level context: A discursive approach, *The International Journal of Human Resource Management*, 31: 474–510.

3 A kaleidoscope of 'talent' definitions and conceptualisations

Introduction

Understanding what talent is, or is not, is vital to the study and practice of talent management. This is because how stakeholders use the term 'talent' in everyday discourses and conversations is the foundation of talent management practice. While there is no denying that all employees are valuable in their own right (otherwise, why hire them?), talent management asserts that specific individuals or groups are of greater value by way of their contribution to the strategic objectives. To practice talent management organisations need to decide the defining characteristics of the talent subject, with stakeholders needing to establish informed understanding of who and what warrants disproportionate investment to ensure commercial viability, operational functionality and strategy execution.

This chapter begins by recognising that talent is a socially and discursively constructed concept with talent meanings arising from talk and processes of negotiation, with numerous stakeholders playing a role in shaping the defining characteristics of a talent subject (i.e. the individual). We then provide an overview of the various explanations and conceptualisations in the literature. Specifically, we set out four dominant ways to think about 'talent':

1 specific individuals.
2 skills and capabilities.
3 pivotal roles and positions.
4 everyone is talent.

The chapter shows the inherent variation whereby some meanings are accepted, while others are contested. While these talent meanings differ in their focus, we note that conceptualisations are not mutually exclusive. Organisations can enact talent management on numerous, rather than a single, understandings of the defining characteristics of talent. In so doing, we show that both scholars and practitioners have several options from which to select, thus creating a situation whereby there is no right way or one way to understand talent. The chapter concedes that while informed talent meanings lay the foundation for effective talent management practices, many scholars fail to define what talent is and means within publications. The absence of a specific term definition, combined with assumptions that stakeholders know (and agree on) what we mean when talking about talent, limits a more informed understanding of the phenomena.

Key chapter take-aways

*   Talent is a socially and discursively constructed concept.
*   Individuals, teams, units, functions, and organisations are required to negotiate what talent is or is not within their specific and strategic context.
*   Organisations and researchers need to be cautious in assuming shared meaning and understanding of common terms.
*   Organisationally based talent meanings can frame talent as all workers and employees whereby everyone is talent, specifically designated individuals, specifically designated skills and capabilities, specifically designated jobs, roles and positions.
*   A spectrum of talent is needed to make the world go 'round' so it is important for organisations to look left, look right, look up and look down.

Talent is – a socially and discursively constructed concept

Studying talent management is complex because talent is a socially constructed idea whose meaning is not standardised, self-explanatory or obvious. While talent is defined in the Oxford dictionary as "natural ability or skill" (p. 926), talent meanings are not found in dictionaries or lexicons. As researchers, we cannot undertake a series of experiments to see what talent means, or prove whether precise definitions exist, and if one is better than another. Instead, social groups decide – and socially construct – what talent means within their context of social history.

Tansley's (2011) consideration of the etymology illustrates how the use of the term has varied over time, having transitioned from a monetary unit in the 13th century to being indicative of treasure and riches in the 15th century. This evolved within Western societies to being more related to a person of talent or ability (Gallardo-Gallardo, Dries & González-Cruz, 2013; Tansley, 2011). References to talent in the 17th century related to a special natural ability or aptitudes and faculties of various kinds (mental orders of a superior order, mental power, or ability). The 19th century experienced a repositioning of talk about talent in relation to an individual whereby talent was viewed as embodied within a person (i.e. the talented). Currently, the term, while mostly referring to specific individuals, is also used as a generic term to describe an individual's ability, accomplishments, aptitudes, brilliance, capacity, expertise, facility, flair, genius, gift, ingenuity, knack, prowess, skill and/or strength. As per the consideration of the evolution of talent meanings over time, what this illustrates is that talent has not been a particularly static concept. Instead, understandings of what talent is (and is not) are malleable and subject to change.

Talent meanings can be expected to vary across individuals, groups and organisations, sometimes converging and sometimes diverging because talent is a discursive concept. Discursive concepts are constructions "through which we understand the world and relate to one another" (Phillips & Hardy, 1997, p. 167). Talent (and talent management) meanings exist as ideas (Hardy & Phillips, 2004; Wiblen & McDonnell, 2020) and arise via the language we use to communicate our perceptions of 'talent' through our internalised schemes and frames, everyday talk and conversations, texts, policies and so on. That is, talent is a concept which only exists in our minds until we communicate meanings and understandings through words and language.

When it comes to talent, as with all socially and discursively constructed concepts (e.g. love, beauty, confidence, leadership, climate change, social distancing), those meanings that prevail will be revealed by the discourses that influence which constructions are 'ruled in' as acceptable (Meriläinen, Tienari, Thomas & Davies, 2004) meanings, and which are 'ruled out', or framed as less legitimate (Hall, 2001; Heracleous, 2006; Phillips, Lawrence & Hardy, 2004). Thus, discourses "do not just describe things; they *do* things" (Potter & Wetherell, 1987, p. 6) and discursive concepts "may well redefine and transform the world to which it is applied" (Grant & Nyberg, 2014, p. 195). Studying the language and meaning embodied in both scholarly and practical discourses will shape how organisations and HR professionals approach/model strategic workforce planning because we all use language, and call upon numerous discourses, to communicate what we mean when talking about talent. Within the context of the study of organisations, researchers may be best advised to not focus on discovering one definition of talent.

Organisations do not *have* a definition of talent but instead they *create* or *establish* talent meanings. In other words, organisations must decide – and socially construct – what talent means within the context of their own operational needs and strategic imperatives. It is also important to not fall into the trap of assuming that because a term is used that this equates to a shared meaning. Examination of the talent concept commences with a consideration of meanings at the individual level. A foundational question is: what does the term talent mean to you? Wiblen and Boudreau (2019), when asking a group of senior HR leaders to share their answer to this question, garnered an array of definitions, including:

- the high-potential employees who are identified for significant advancement.
- the inherent capability that exists in each of our employees.
- the competencies that we identify in our internal system.
- the capacity that our employees have to do their job.

Understanding the meanings that underpin the talk about talent has implications within societies and organisations. Specifically, how leaders communicate and think about talent will influence how they manage (and reward) the internal talent pool. Furthermore, how we attribute meaning to talent has implications for how we practice talent management, measure performance and potential, and establish the defining characteristics of talented individuals (Boudreau, 2019; Meyers, van Woerkom, Paauwe & Dries, 2020).

Talent is – influenced by various stakeholders and context

Multiple stakeholders have a role in socially and discursively constructing talent meanings. Questions about who decides what talent is involves garnering an informed understanding of the stakeholders with power and agency over talent meanings. Certain stakeholders will seek to have their ideas and perspectives deemed most legitimate. This stakeholder influence can be covert and/or overt. Not all voices are equally represented within and between organisations, with potential for talent meanings to arise outside of an organisation. Table 3.1 provides an overview of the various stakeholders who need to be considered when reflecting on where talent meanings come from and the actors who may influence the social construction of talent within organisational boundaries. We suggest such consideration as being especially important in improving the recognition that talent is a contested terrain and one where a plurality of interests exist and interact.

The ideas of talent and the language employed to construct what talent means socially and discursively within organisations are influenced by factors that are specific to their operational and strategic context. Consideration of context – the situational opportunities and constraints that affect the occurrence and meaning of organisational behaviour as well as functional relationships between variables (Johns, 2006, p. 386) – is important in making sense of what is happening in the rich world of reality (Cooke, 2017) and within organisational boundaries specifically. Recognising the

Table 3.1 Stakeholders shaping talent meanings

Stakeholder	Potential role in shaping talent meanings
Academics	Prescribe what talent should and could be.
Consultants	Focus on defining and providing problem-based and solution-driven client-based services for financial gain.
Senior stakeholders	Establish the short- and long-term direction of the organisation and the associated workforce and talent needs.
HR personnel and professionals	Play a role in establishing, enacting and enforcing performance and talent management frameworks.
Line managers	Responsible for day-to-day management and evaluation of individuals at the team level.
Customers	Establish demand for services and can evaluate the performance of client-based or task-based work.
Unions	Focus on the needs of the entire workforce and can shape internal workforce practices and to whom they apply.
Admired CEO or business guru	Share and consume innovative ideas assuming replication.
Technology vendors	Provide technology-embedded frameworks for mapping the workforce (e.g. the nine-box matrix).
Leadership capability frameworks	Present predetermined/composed frameworks for mapping individuals against certain leadership capabilities.
Competency models	Provide predetermined/composed frameworks for mapping individuals against certain competencies.

influence and impact of context is salient because talent management is a complex multilevel phenomenon.

Reflection on the contextual nature of talent is vital. The connection between talent and country-based contexts is highlighted in two books *Macro Talent Management: A Global Perspective on Managing Talent in Developed Markets* and *Macro Talent Management in Emerging and Emergent Markets: A Global Perspective* edited by Vaiman, Sparrow, Schuler and Collings (2018a, b). The salience of context is reinforced in an *International Journal of Human Resource Management* Special Issue dedicated to context (Gallardo-Gallardo, Thunnissen & Scullion, 2020). Featured papers illustrate the expansive and pervasive role of context in talent management phenomena (see Asplund, 2020; Meyers et al., 2020; Sumelius, Smale & Yamao, 2020; Wiblen & McDonnell, 2020). Through more contextualised perspectives, talent management research can help scholars bridge the gap between academia and practice because talent management (and thus talent meanings) cannot be understood as a stand-alone phenomenon since it is designed and implemented in an organisation.

In this regard, Meyers et al. (2020), in building on previous work (Meyers & van Woerkom, 2014) advocate the importance of considering the underpinning talent philosophies. Suggesting that HR managers have different beliefs about whether talent is an exclusive or inclusive concept, or whether talent is stable (innate) or developable (acquirable), the authors test the presence of four distinct talent philosophies: exclusive/innate; exclusive/developable; inclusive/innate; and inclusive/developable and the impact of organisational context (i.e. size, ownership form, multinational orientation) on each. Results of an online survey of 321 HR managers from various countries indicated an equal prevalence of the four philosophies. The findings indicate that while scholars tend to disproportionately advocate for a more exclusive-type concept whereby some individuals are of keen focus over all staff, the same assumptions may not resonate with practitioners. The results demonstrate that talent philosophies are influenced by country, organisational size and organisational approach to talent management, suggesting that some of the study participants shaped the definitions and practices within their respective workplaces. In this regard, scholars may look to the international and comparative HRM scholarship which has a strong history in considering contextual influences on practice (e.g. Brewster, Mayrhofer & Smale, 2016; Budhwar & Sparrow, 2002; Dewettinck & Remue, 2011)

Wiblen and McDonnell (2020) similarly highlight the influence of contextual factors and variables on talent meanings using a discourse analysis of 79 in-depth interviews of key internal stakeholders of a professional services' firm. This study illustrated how societal, institutional, phenomenological, organisational, localised and individual factors influenced talent concepts. The authors argued that:

> talent can only be examined within a specific context, at a specific point of time, from specific individual perspectives. We cannot infer, furthermore, that talent meanings radiate within organisations, nor across organisational boundaries, industries or countries because discourses [the talk about what talent is or is not] arise and materialise within specific contexts and we must acknowledge that talent discourses cannot be removed from the context in which they operate.
>
> (Wiblen & McDonnell, 2020, p. 477)

Talent conceptualisations

Everyday talk about talent illuminates how discourse shapes social reality (Grant & Nyberg, 2014). For each definition proposed in the field, authors are seeking to shape conversations by offering their individual, team or function-based perspective of what talent means to them or prescribe how we should talk about talent (Wiblen & McDonnell, 2020). Within this section we highlight several talent definitions (see Table 3.2) to illustrate how scholars associate the term with four main concepts:

1 all workers, skills and capabilities whereby *everyone is talent*.
2 specifically designated *individuals*.
3 specifically designated *skills and capabilities*.
4 specifically designated (e.g. pivotal) *jobs, roles or positions*.

Talent as all workers and employees

A significant but disregarded perspective in the field asserts that all individuals within a workforce are talent. This is in spite of concerns that merit systems are flawed and can reduce motivation (Blass & April, 2008; Gladwell, 2002), while there is also much research that advocates for inclusive and diverse workplaces (Gallardo-Gallardo & Thunnissen, 2016). The 'everyone as talent' concept champions inclusive-subject, inclusive-object (Thunnissen, Boselie & Fruytier, 2013a), as well as inclusivity-based conceptualisations, while actively refuting notions of exclusivity and workforce differentiation. Although organisations can and should make predictive judgments about the current and future value of individuals before they join the organisation, this perspective suggests no further distinction should take place post-selection. Advocates believe that all employees encompass the talents that the organisation requires. The talent inherent in each of these individuals underpins the primary reasoning for why they have been selected as employees of the organisation. Consequently, talent status is something automatically allocated upon selection, rather than any internal review, performance evaluation or identification process that occurs while in employment (Wiblen & McDonnell, 2020). In addition, each individual will demonstrate a certain level of potential which the organisation will seek to develop and utilise.

Scholars and practitioners often recognise that it is commendable for organisations to profess that all humans are talent and equally valuable, and provide a high baseline of investment and support to all, but also that it is wise for organisations to invest resources differentially (unequally) to achieve the greatest stakeholder value (Collings, McDonnell & McMackin, 2017; Collings, McDonnell & Scullion, 2009).

Table 3.2 Examples of talent definitions and conceptualisations

Talent definition/meaning; definitions and understandings of talent	Source	Explicit or implied talent meanings	Exclusive versus inclusive meaning (implicit or explicit)	Talent meaning discourse
From a human capital perspective, talent refers to the human capital in an organisation that is both valuable and unique, with an *employee's* contribution to the organisation the main criterion of interest.	Dries (2013, p. 276)	Individuals	Inclusive and Exclusive	Individuals Everyone is talent
Talent refers to systematically developed innate abilities of *individuals* who are deployed in activities they like, find important and in which they want to invest energy. It enables individuals to perform excellently in one or more domains of human functioning, operationalised as performing better than other individuals of the same age of experience, or as performing consistently at their personal best.	Nijs, Gallardo-Gallardo, Dries and Sels (2014, p. 182)	Individuals	Exclusive	Individuals
Subject perspectives on talent imply a focus on the identification and development of *talented people.*	Dries (2013, p. 278)	Individuals Characteristics of individuals	Exclusive	Individuals
Object perspectives on talent, on the other hand, imply a focus on the identification and development of *characteristics of* talented people.				

(Continued)

Table 3.2 (Continued)

Talent definition/meaning: definitions and understandings of talent	Source	Explicit or implied talent meanings	Exclusive versus inclusive meaning (implicit or explicit)	Talent meaning discourse
Talent can be an innate construct which is mostly acquired or results from the interaction between (specific levels of) nature and nurture components. 1 Talent is innate (nature): whereby *talented employees* are endowed with certain qualities, while others are not. 2 Talent is acquired (nurture): whereby the value of employees can be enhanced.	Meyers, van Woerkom and Dries (2013)	Individuals Individuals with certain attributes	Exclusive	Individuals
Talent has been used broadly to describe an *individual's* skill, aptitude and achievement. The four elements of individual talent are potency (person's power, influence and capability to achieve results), truest interest (passion), skill intelligences (mental and physical learning and performance abilities to compete, conquer and survive) and virtue intelligence (moral excellence and integrity).	van Dijk (2008, p. 387)	Individuals	Inclusive	Everybody is talent
Talent is the resource that includes the potential and realised capacities of *individuals*.	van Dijk (2009)	Individuals with certain attributes Individuals	Inclusive	Everybody is talent
We define talent as the resource that includes the potential and realised capacities of *individuals* and groups and how they are organised, including those within the organisation and those who might join the organisation.	Boudreau and Ramstad (2007, p. 2)	Individuals Groups of individuals	Inclusive (individuals) and Exclusive (certain groups)	Individuals Everyone is talent

Talent consists of those *individuals* who can make a difference to organisational performance, either through their immediate contribution or in the longer term by demonstrating the highest levels of potential.	CIPD (2007, p. 3)	Individuals	Exclusive	Individuals
Talent refers to a select group of *employees*, those who rank at the top in terms of capability and performance, rather than the entire workforce.	Stahl et al. (2007, p. 4)	Individuals	Exclusive	Individuals
There is a commonly held perception of a global war for talent, in which organisations must fiercely compete with other employers for a finite supply of desperately needed *workers*, especially those with hard-to-find or highly valued skills, including leadership skills.	Wellins and Schweyer (2007, p. 2)	Individuals Individuals with certain skills	Exclusive	Everyone is talent Skills and capabilities
Talent is an inherent *individual* quality to be sought out and recruited.	MacBeath (2006, p. 183)	Individual	Inclusive	Everyone is talent
Talent is the sum of a *person's* abilities; his or her intrinsic gifts, *skills*, knowledge, experience, intelligence, judgment, attitude, character and drive. It also includes his or her ability to grow.	Michaels, Handfield-Jones and Axelrod (2001, p. xii)	Individuals Individuals with ceratin attributes Individuals with certain skills	Inclusive	Individuals Everyone is talent Skills and capabilities
Talent should refer to a *person's* recurring patterns of thought, feelings or behaviour that can be productively applied. By this definition, impatience is a talent, as are charm, strategic thinking, competitiveness, empathy, focus and tact. According to the most common sense and the most arcane neuroscience, talents such as these are enduring and unique. They are almost impossible to teach.	Buckingham and Vosburgh (2001)	Individuals Individuals with certain attributes	Inclusive	Individuals

(Continued)

Table 3.2 (Continued)

Talent definition/meaning; definitions and understandings of talent	Source	Explicit or implied talent meanings	Exclusive versus inclusive meaning (implicit or explicit)	Talent meaning discourse
Some key *technical employees* may legitimately be classified as talent in some organisations.	McDonnell, Lamare, Gunnigle and Lavelle (2010, p. 158)	Individuals Individuals with certain (technical) skills	Exclusive	Individuals Skills and capabilities
Talent is concerned with identifying *key positions* which have the potential to differentially impact the firm's competitive advantage and filling these with 'A performers'.	Whelen and Carcary (2011, p. 676)	Pivotal positions	Exclusive	Pivotal roles and positions
There may be functional and technical type *roles* which have a sizeable strategic impact on the organisation.	McDonnell (2011)	Pivotal roles	Exclusive	Pivotal roles and positions
It has never been more important to have talented employees staff the organisation's key *strategic positions.*	McDonnell et al. (2010, p. 150)	Strategic positions	Exclusive	Individuals Pivotal roles and positions
Pivotal talent pools are the vital targets for HR investment and leader attention.	Boudreau and Ramstad (2005b, p. 129)	Pivotal talent pools	Exclusive	Pivotal roles and positions

Source: Wiblen and McDonnell (2020, pp. 478–480)

Talent as specifically designated individuals

Despite definitional and language-based differences, most current talent management and HRM texts assume that talent is a term applied to either a specifically designated individual or a group of specifically designated individuals (a talent pool). Thus, there is evidence of some degree of convergence that talent is an exclusive concept.

Most scholars are proponents of exclusive-type conceptualisations and practices prioritising workforce differentiation (Gallardo-Gallardo & Thunnissen, 2016; McDonnell, Collings, Mellahi & Schuler, 2017). Associated with an exclusive perspective are assertions that talent is an individualistic concept with Western perceptions emphasising an above-average individual who can perform to their ability in a given domain (Gagné, 2004; Gallardo-Gallardo et al., 2013; Nijs et al., 2014; Tansley, 2011). Tansley (2011) notes talented individuals either: exhibit certain behaviours deemed valuable, or are evaluated as a high performer, and/or possessing high potential or certain strengths. Nijs et al. (2014), post-integration of insights from positive psychology, vocational psychology, giftedness literature and HRM, propose that:

> Talent refers to systematically developed innate abilities of *individuals* [emphasis added] that are deployed in activities they like, find important, and in which they want to invest energy. It enables individuals to perform excellently in one or more domains of human functioning, operationalised as performing better than other individuals of the same age of experience, or as performing consistently at their personal best.
>
> (p. 182)

Many studies attribute great importance to the identification and retention of key (some) individuals. These individuals are seen to be of greater value because they contribute more to the organisation's business activities and overall success (Deloitte, 2008a). Individualistic talent concepts are also inferred in discourses attesting to the importance of high-performing and high-potential individuals (Michaels et al., 2001; Stahl et al., 2007), rising stars, top talent and/or future leaders. This approach maintains that such individuals have the potential to reach high levels of achievement (Tansley, 2011) and are potentially representative of the next generation of organisational leaders (Collings & Mellahi, 2009; Mäkelä, Björkman & Ehrnrooth, 2010; McDonnell et al., 2010; Stahl et al., 2007). Indeed, McDonnell et al.'s (2017) systematic review of the academic landscape confirmed a preference for the idea that talent refers to specific individuals – usually high performers and high potentials – with existing empirical and conceptual publications avouching this perspective.

Notably and usefully, discussions about whether talent is innate or acquired (Collings & Mellahi, 2013; Meyers et al., 2013; Nijs et al., 2014) do not require reconciliation as both perspectives reside within this dominant discourse. Similarly, the 'talent-as-object' and 'talent-as-subject' (Dries, 2013; Gallardo-Gallardo et al., 2013) approaches do not consciously or unconsciously give meaning to talent in non-individualistic and non-human-centric ways. These papers are especially useful starting points for gaining a more in-depth appreciation of how talent is treated across different disciplines.

Talent as specifically designated skills and capabilities

Proclamations of the value of specific skills and capabilities operate in academic and praxis discourses alongside the dominant 'individuals as talent' perspective. The 'skills and capabilities' perspective asserts that specific skills and capabilities are critical to operational processes, strategic direction and organisational performance (Wiblen, Dery & Grant, 2012; Wiblen, Grant & Dery, 2010). This category includes individuals or teams which possess skills and capabilities (including capacity and ability) of value because they are required to drive future growth (Deloitte, 2008b) and/or are hard to replace (CIPD, 2006; McDonnell et al., 2010). This category can include cohorts of employees such as knowledge workers, professional services staff and/or technical experts (April & Jappie, 2008; Blass, 2007; Lah, 2009; McDonnell et al., 2016). More recently, we have witnessed a somewhat expanded discourse with an increasing emphasis on analytics-based and evidence-based skills (Barends, Rousseau & Briner, 2014; J. Boudreau & Jesuthasan, 2011; Marler & Boudreau, 2017; Pfeffer & Sutton, 2006) to go with the long-standing knowledge work domain.

Talent status determinations are therefore founded on the skills and capabilities that the individual holds, rather than the individual per se. While organisations that materialise the 'some individuals as talent' concept will debate the extent to which they prioritise developing generic or technical skills and/or competencies (Claussen, Grohsjean, Luger & Probst, 2014; Garavan, Hogan & Cahir-O'Donnell, 2009; Siikaniemi, 2012) of a specific individual, this perspective values the unique skills and capabilities confined within the individual. Specific skills and capabilities are the defining talent characteristic (Wiblen & McDonnell, 2020) with the individuals themselves substitutable. Specificity about which skills and capabilities are important will/should change in line with strategic objectives.

Talent as specifically designated jobs, roles and positions

The likelihood that an individual is talent may also depend on the position they hold or role that they play. Founded on the seminal work of Boudreau and Ramstad (2005a, b), this talent concept asserts that particular functions and roles are pivotal or critical to strategic success. This perspective suggests that the practice of talent management should start with the identification of pivotal roles (Boudreau & Ramstad, 2005a, b) rather than of individual employees or specific skills and capabilities. Organisations are encouraged to identify and allocate appropriate employees to these specific roles (see Collings & Mellahi, 2009; Mellahi & Collings, 2010). Investing in these roles is argued as what will make a significant strategic difference (Boudreau & Ramstad, 2007).

Valuable and strategic positions, frequently inferred in definitions of talent management (for example see Collings & Mellahi, 2009; Mellahi & Collings, 2010), are those where small incremental improvements in quality and quantity result in above-average returns. It is the investment in these roles, or 'A positions' (Huselid, Beatty & Becker, 2005), which can aid with a competitive advantage (Boudreau & Ramstad, 2007). In turn, organisations may segment their workforce into key talent pools (Boudreau & Ramstad, 2005b) and post a systematic analysis of their business (Wiblen et al., 2012; Wiblen et al., 2010). While all roles facilitate the fulfilment of operational imperatives, not all roles contribute equally to strategy execution. Relevant stakeholders will determine which roles and positions are valuable, pivotal and strategic.

The most pivotal roles in organisations may not be those which one thinks of first. For example, how would you respond when asked who is 'talent' at Disneyland (the theme parks)? It is not, as one might think, the people who dress up as Disney characters. Rather, Boudreau and Ramstad (2007), after a study of pivotal roles and positions in Disneyland, reported that street sweepers are the most pivotal talent as it this group of individuals who interact the most with park patrons and have the most significant impact on the customer's experience. Street sweepers do more than just keep the park clean. Individuals in these roles provide information about the best vantage points to view the parades, share information about toilet facilities and give directions to rides and other park amenities. Street sweepers are pivotal because they contribute disproportionately to the execution of Disneyland's motto – The Happiest Place on Earth (Wiblen, 2019).

Talent as an undefined concept

Although there is a prescriptive assumption that talent should be defined, an array of publications on talent management appear to take for granted this central concept (e.g. Boudreau & Ramstad, 2005a; Calo, 2008; Capelli,

2008; Frank & Taylor, 2004; Guthridge, Komm & Lawson, 2008; Joerres & Turcq, 2007; Lah, 2009; Warren, 2009), or fail to define it (Gallardo-Gallardo et al., 2013; Thunnissen & Gallardo-Gallardo, 2019). McDonnell (2011) and Tansley (2011) both highlight how numerous publications about talent management fail to state how talent is defined, with Gallardo-Gallardo and Thunnissen (2016) suggesting that a mere 16 per cent of papers explicitly specified how talent was treated within published research studies. This is problematic given the varied perspectives and meanings that the talent concept can take. Without clarity on how studies treat the concept, it will be impossible to make appropriate interpretations of the empirical base.

The absence of more empirically informed-based discussions about talent in the literature is somewhat perplexing given the inherent requirement for organisations to operationalise a definition of talent to enact talent management. Nijs et al.'s (2014) notion that "robust theory building and accurate interpretation of empirical data cannot take place until formal definitions are established" (p. 180) firmly applies given the centrality of talent to the practice of talent management. Indeed, given the concept's poor treatment and limited clarity provided leads one to question the usefulness of using the word talent in the corporate lexicon. Tansley (2011, p. 267) asks about the relevance of the term 'talent' at all. Why not use any other human resourcing term, such as 'skills' or 'knowledge' or 'competencies'?

Conclusion

Talent as an undefined concept whereby researchers fail to define what they mean within the context of their discussions and publications is not an inconsequential limitation. Rather, the failure is a core limitation of the literature. While we assert that there is no correct way to define talent, we believe that it is imperative that scholars and practitioners explicitly declare their approach when contributing to the conversations, debates and knowledge. Informed understandings of what talent means (definitions) and is (defining characteristics) are the baselines for talent management practices. Relevant stakeholders may transition from talent as an idea into action through specific practices and, vice versa, because of the potentially dual effect of discourses and the relationship between an 'idea' and 'practice' and 'talk' and 'action' (Vaara, Kleymann & Seristö, 2004).

Organisations, via relevant stakeholders, need to establish talent meanings within the context of their strategic goals and in doing so can select from one or more of the conceptualisations profiled in this chapter – individuals, skills and capabilities, designated jobs, roles and positions, or all workers and employees whereby everyone is talent. The many definitions, conceptualisations and typologies currently offered are suggestions of what individuals and organisations could mean when they talk about talent. As such this complicates, rather than clarifies, our understanding of what talent means and is. Although the various and, at times, contradictory beliefs of the talent concept come as little surprise, a core limitation of this scholarship is the assumption that everyone knows (and agrees on) what we are talking about when we talk about talent (Wiblen & McDonnell, 2019, p. 1). The absence of explicit meanings is a core limitation and presents a weak and negligent foundation for both the study and practice of talent management.

The intention of scholars should not be to reconcile divergent perspectives nor to seek convergence. Pluralistic considerations of what happens in the world of practice, as well as an examination of who is considered talent and why (Gallardo-Gallardo et al., 2013, p. 290), are the keys to better informed understandings. Appreciating the complexity of talent is key because, while stakeholders may talk about it in the same way, they may mean different things and have different views of a what a talented individual 'looks like' (the defining characteristics) and what talented subjects do (how they act). Researchers and practitioners alike would benefit from explicitly recognising that talent definitions and conceptualisations cannot be removed from the context in which talent is situated (Meyers et al., 2020; Nijs et al., 2014; Thunnissen, Boselie & Fruytier, 2013b; Wiblen & McDonnell, 2020).

References

April, K. & Jappie, A. (2008). Global talent warfare: Line managers are still the determinant, *Journal for Convergence*, 9: 40–43.

Asplund, K. (2020). When profession trumps potential: The moderating role of professional identification in employees' reactions to talent management, *The International Journal of Human Resource Management*, 31: 539–561.

Barends, E., Rousseau, D. & Briner, R. (2014). *Evidence-based Management: The Basic Principals*, Amsterdam: Center for Evidence-Based Management.

Blass, E. (2007). *Talent Management: Maximising Talent for Business Performance. Executive Summary November 2007*. Retrieved from London: www.ashridge.org. uk/Website/IC.nsf/wFARPUB/Talent+Management:+Maximising+talent+for+b usiness+performance?opendocument

Blass, E. & April, K. (2008). Developing talent for tomorrow, *Develop*, 1: 48–58.

Boudreau, J. W. (2019). *The Future HR: Five Essential But Overlooked Questions*. Retrieved from: https://ceo.usc.edu/2019/08/20/the-future-hr-five-essential-but-overlooked-questions-the-future-hr-five-essential-but-overlooked-questions/

Boudreau, J. W. & Jesuthasan, R. (2011). *Transformative HR: How Great Companies Use Evidence Based Change for Sustainable Competitive Advantage*, San Francisco: Jossey Bass.

Boudreau, J. W. & Ramstad, P. M. (2005a). Talentship and the new paradigm for human resource management: From professional practices to strategic talent decision science, *Human Resource Planning*, 28: 17–26.

Boudreau, J. W. & Ramstad, P. M. (2005b). Talentship, talent segmentation, and sustainability: A new HR decision science paradigm for a new strategy definition, *Human Resource Management*, 44: 129–136.

Boudreau, J. W. & Ramstad, P. M. (2007). *Beyond HR: The New Science of Human Capital,* Boston, MA: Harvard Business School Press.

Brewster, C., Mayrhofer, W. & Smale, A. (2016). Crossing the streams: HRM in multinational enterprises and comparative HRM, *Human Resource Management Review,* 26: 285–297.

Buckingham, M. & Vosburgh, R. M. (2001). The 21st century human resources function: It's the talent, stupid! *Human Resource Planning,* 24: 17–23.

Budhwar, P. & Sparrow, P. (2002). An integrative framework for understanding cross-national human resource management practices, *Human Resource Management Review,* 12: 377–403.

Calo, T. J. (2008). Talent management in the era of the aging workforce: The critical role of knowledge transfer, *Public Personnel Management,* 37: 403–416.

Capelli, P. (2008). Talent management for the twenty-first century, *Harvard Business Review,* 86: 74–81.

CIPD. (2006). *Talent Management: Understanding the Dimensions.* Retrieved from London: www.cipd.co.uk/subjects/recruitmen/general/_tlmtmgtdim. htm?IsSrchRes=1

CIPD (2007). *Talent: Strategy, Management, Measurement.* London: CIPD.

Claussen, J., Grohsjean, T., Luger, J. & Probst, G. (2014). Talent management and career development: What it takes to get promoted, *Journal of World Business,* 49: 236–244.

Collings, D. G., McDonnell, A. & McMackin, J. (2017). Talent management, in P. Sparrow & C. Cooper (Eds.), *A Research Agenda for Human Resource Management,* Cheltenham: Edward Elgar Publishing, pp. 39–54.

Collings, D. G., McDonnell, A. & Scullion, H. (2009). Global talent management: The law of the few, *Poznan University of Economics Review,* 9: 5–18.

Collings, D. G. & Mellahi, K. (2009). Strategic talent management: A review and research agenda, *Human Resource Management Review,* 19: 304–313.

Collings, D. G. & Mellahi, K. (2013). Commentary on: "Talent – Innate or acquired? Theoretical considerations and their implications for talent management", *Human Resource Management Review,* 23: 322–325.

Cooke, F. L. (2017). Concepts, contexts, and mindsets: Putting human resource management research in perspectives, *Human Resource Management Journal,* 28: 1–13.

Deloitte. (2008a). The chemistry of talent: New ways to think about people and work, *Straight Talk Book No. 10.* Retrieved from: www.deloitte.com.mx/documents/mx(en-mx)TheChemistryTalent_24ago09.pdf

Deloitte. (2008b). *It's 2008: Do You Know Where Your Talent Is? Why Acquisition and Retention Strategies Don't Work.* Retrieved from: http://oportunidades. deloitte.cl/marketing/Archivos%20en%20la%20web/Crisis%20de%20talento%20en%20la%20industria%20manufacturera.pdf

Dewettinck, K. & Remue, J. (2011). Contextualising HRM in comparative research: The role of the Cranet network, *Human Resource Management Review,* 21: 37–49.

Dries, N. (2013). The psychology of talent management: A review and research agenda, *Human Resource Management Review,* 23: 272–285.

Frank, F. D. & Taylor, C. R. (2004). Talent management: Trends that will shape the future, *Human Resource Planning,* 27: 33–41.

Gagné, F. (2004). Transforming gifts into talents: The DMGT as a developmental theory, *High Ability Studies,* 15: 119–147.

Gallardo-Gallardo, E., Dries, N. & González-Cruz, T. F. (2013). What is the meaning of "talent" in the world of work? *Human Resource Management Review*, 23: 290–300.

Gallardo-Gallardo, E. & Thunnissen, M. (2016). Standing on the shoulders of giants? A critical review of empirical talent management research, *Employee Relations*, 38: 31–56.

Gallardo-Gallardo, E., Thunnissen, M. & Scullion, H. (2020). Talent management: Context matters, *The International Journal of Human Resource Management*, 31: 457–473.

Garavan, T. N., Hogan, C. & Cahir-O'Donnell, A. (2009). *Developing Managers and Leaders: Perspectives, Debates and Practices in Ireland*, Dublin: Gill Education.

Gladwell, M. (2002). The talent myth: Are smart people overrated? *The New Yorker*, July 22: 28–33.

Grant, D. & Nyberg, D. (2014). Business and the communication of climate change: An organisational discourse perspective, in V. Bhatia & S. Bremner (Eds.), *The Routledge Handbook of Language and Professional Communication*, London: Taylor & Francis Ltd, pp. 193–206.

Guthridge, M., Komm, A. B. & Lawson, E. (2008). Making talent a strategic priority, *The McKinsey Quarterly*, 1: 49–59.

Hall, S. (2001). Foucault: Power, knowledge and discourse, in M. Wetherell, S. Taylor & S. J. Yates (Eds.), *Discourse Theory and Practice: A Reader*, London: SAGE Publications, pp. 72–81.

Hardy, C. & Phillips, N. (2004). Discourse and power, in D. Grant, C. Hardy, C. Oswick & L. Putnam (Eds.), *Handbook of Organizational Discourse*, London: SAGE Publications, pp. 299–316.

Heracleous, L. (2006). A tale of three discourses: The dominant, the strategic and the marginalised, *Journal of Management Studies*, 43: 1059–1087.

Huselid, M. A., Beatty, R. W. & Becker, B. E. (2005). "A players" or "A positions"? The strategic logic of workforce management, *Harvard Business Review*, December: 110–117.

Joerres, J. & Turcq, D. (2007). Talent value management, *Industrial Management*, 49: 8–13.

Johns, G. (2006). The essential impact of context on organisational behavior, *The Academy of Management Review*, 31: 386–408.

Lah, T. E. (2009). Using talent supply chain management to overcome challenges in the professional services market, *Workforce Management*, 88: 1–10.

Mäkelä, K., Björkman, I. & Ehrnrooth, M. (2010). How do MNCs establish their talent pools? Influences on individuals' likelihood of being labeled as talent, *Journal of World Business*, 45: 134–142.

Marler, J. H. & Boudreau, J. W. (2017). An evidence-based review of HR analytics, *The International Journal of Human Resource Management*, 28: 3–26.

MacBeath, J. (2006). The talent enigma. *International Journal of Leadership in Education*, 9: 183–204.

McDonnell, A., Gunnigle, P., Lavelle, J. & Lamare, R. (2016). Beyond managerial and leadership elites: "Key group" identification and differential reward architectures in multinational companies, *The International Journal of Human Resource Management*, 27: 1299–1318.

McDonnell, A. (2011). Still fighting the war for talent? Bridging the science versus practice gap, *Journal of Business and Psychology*, 26: 169–173.

McDonnell, A., Collings, D. G., Mellahi, K. & Schuler, R. (2017). Talent management: A systematic review and future prospects, *European Journal of International Management*, 11: 86–128.

McDonnell, A., Lamare, R., Gunnigle, P. & Lavelle, J. (2010). Developing tomorrow's leaders- evidence of global talent management in multinational companies, *Journal of World Business*, 45: 150–160.

Mellahi, K. & Collings, D. G. (2010). The barriers to effective global talent management: The example of corporate élites in MNEs, *Journal of World Business*, 45: 143–149.

Meriläinen, S., Tienari, J., Thomas, R. & Davies, A. (2004). Management consultant talk: A cross-cultural comparison of normalizing discourse and resistance, *Organization*, 11: 539–564.

Meyers, M. C. & van Woerkom, M. (2014). The influence of underlying philosophies on talent management: Theory, implications for practice, and research agenda, *Journal of World Business*, 49: 192–203.

Meyers, M. C., van Woerkom, M. & Dries, N. (2013). Talent – Innate or acquired? Theoretical considerations and their implications for talent management, *Human Resource Management Review*, 23: 305–321.

Meyers, M. C., van Woerkom, M., Paauwe, J. & Dries, N. (2020). HR managers' talent philosophies: Prevalence and relationships with perceived talent management practices, *The International Journal of Human Resource Management*, 31: 562–588.

Michaels, E., Handfield-Jones, H. & Axelrod, B. (2001). *The War for Talent*, Boston: Harvard Business School Press.

Nijs, S., Gallardo-Gallardo, E., Dries, N. & Sels, L. (2014). A multidisciplinary review into the definition, operationalisation, and measurement of talent, *Journal of World Business*, 49: 180–191.

Pfeffer, J. & Sutton, R. I. (2006). *Hard Facts, Dangerous Half-Truths and Total Nonsense: Profiting from Evidence-Based management*, Boston: Harvard Business School Press.

Phillips, N. & Hardy, C. (1997). Managing multiple identities: Discourse, legitimacy and resources in the UK refugee system, *Organization*, 4: 159–185.

Phillips, N., Lawrence, T. B. & Hardy, C. (2004). Discourse and institutions, *Academy of Management Journal*, 29: 635–652.

Potter, J. & Wetherell, M. (1987). *Discourse and Social Psychology: Beyond Attitudes and Behaviour*, London: Sage Publications.

Siikaniemi, L. (2012). Information pathways for the competence foresight mechanism in talent management framework, *European Journal of Training and Development*, 36: 46–65.

Stahl, G., Björkman, I., Farndale, E., Morris, S. S., Paauwe, J., Stiles, P. & Wright, P. M. (2007). Global talent management: How leading multinationals build and sustain their talent pipeline, *INSEAD Working Papers Collection*, 34: 1–36.

Sumelius, J., Smale, A. & Yamao, S. (2020). Mixed signals: Employee reactions to talent status communication amidst strategic ambiguity, *The International Journal of Human Resource Management*, 31: 511–538.

Tansley, C. (2011). What do we mean by the term "talent" in talent management? *Industrial and Commercial Training*, 43: 266–274.

Thunnissen, M., Boselie, P. & Fruytier, B. (2013a). A review of talent management: "Infancy or adolescence?", *The International Journal of Human Resource Management*, 24: 1744–1761.

Thunnissen, M., Boselie, P. & Fruytier, B. (2013b). Talent management and the relevance of context: Towards a pluralistic approach, *Human Resource Management Review*, 23: 326–336.

Thunnissen, M. & Gallardo-Gallardo, E. (2019). Rigor and relevance in empirical TM research: Key issues and challenges, *BRQ Business Research Quarterly*, 22: 171–180.

Vaara, E., Kleymann, B. & Seristö, H. (2004). Strategies as discursive constructions: The case of airline alliances, *Journal of Management Studies*, 41: 1–35.

Vaiman, V., Sparrow, P., Schuler, R. & Collings, D. G. (Eds.). (2018a). *Macro Talent Management in Emerging and Emergent Markets: A Global Perspective*, New York: Routledge.

Vaiman, V., Sparrow, P., Schuler, R. & Collings, D. G. (Eds.). (2018b). *Macro Talent Management: A Global Perspective on Managing Talent in Developed Markets*, New York: Routledge.

Van Dijk, H.G. (2008). The talent management approach to human resource management: Attracting and retaining the right people, *Journal of Public Administration*, 43: 385–395.

Van Dijk, H. G. (2009). Administration Vs. Talent: The Administrative Context for Talent Management, *Journal of Public Administration*, 44: 520–530.

Warren, A. K. (2009). *Cascading Gender Biases, Compounding Effects: An Assessment of Talent Management Systems*. Retrieved from: www.catalyst.org/publication/292/cascading-gender-biases-compounding-effects-an-assessment-of-talent-management-systems

Wellins, R. S. & Schweyer, A. (2007). *Talent Management in Motion: Keeping Up with an Evolving Workforce*. Pittsburgh, PA: Development Dimensions International Press.

Whelen, E. & Carcary, M. (2011). Integrating talent and knowledge management: where are the benefits? *Journal of Knowledge Management*, 15: 675–687.

Wiblen, S. (2019). e-Talent in talent management, in M. Thite (Ed.), *e-HRM: Digital Approaches, Directions and Applications*, Milton Park: Routledge, pp. 153–171.

Wiblen, S. & Boudreau, J. W. (2019). *Will You Be Ready for 2030 and Beyond? Future-Proofing HR for Talent and Technology Changes*. Paper presented at the Centre for Effective Organizations' 2019 Sponsors' Meeting, Redondo Beach, United States of America.

Wiblen, S., Dery, K. & Grant, D. (2012). Do you see what I see? The role of technology in talent identification, *Asia Pacific Journal of Human Resources*, 50: 421–438.

Wiblen, S., Grant, D. & Dery, K. (2010). Transitioning to a new HRIS: The reshaping of human resources and information technology talent, *Journal of Electronic Commerce Research*, 11: 251–267.

Wiblen, S. & McDonnell, A. (2020). Connecting "talent" meanings and multi-level context: A discursive approach, *The International Journal of Human Resource Management*, 31: 474–510.

4 Talent identification

Understanding how organisations could, should and do identify talent

Introduction

To manage talent effectively, organisations must first identify the talent (Hartmann, Feisel & Schober, 2010) and decide which individuals will receive the additional focus of talent management policies and practices. Furthermore, determining which individuals, or groups of individuals, have specific characteristics (Jooss, Burbach & Ruël, 2019a; Tansley & Tietze, 2013), and consequently a higher value occurs via a specific talent management practice – talent identification. Organisations benefit from engaging in activities which extract value from talent subjects because, as Mellahi and Collings rightful note, the "availability of talent *per se* is of little strategic value if it is not identified" (2010, p. 5). Therefore, talent identification decisions are the foundation for subsequent development and retention practices.

This chapter provides an overview of the various perspectives of how organisations should, could and do make judgments about which individuals are talent. The chapter commences by recognising that talent identification is the practice through which talent meanings 'come to life'. We provide a definition and highlight core attributes before giving an overview of the publications about the processes through which specific individuals are judged and evaluated as being more important than their workforce peers. The chapter profiles the various conceptual viewpoints about how an organisation *could* and *should* endeavour to devise internal talent pools, with most publications saying that systematic, along with evidence- and analytics-based approaches are more effective than ad hoc, intuitive and individualised techniques. The chapter then highlights the findings of what are limited empirical studies that unpack how organisations *do* identify talent. What this evidence indicates is that there is a disconnect between the rhetoric and reality of systematic practices. There are data displaying divergent perspectives about the value of clearly defined criteria and processes for gaining talent status or talent pool admission. Key questions that arise include do you think you know talent when you see it? And do you think that we can qualify and measure talent? The chapter also reminds readers of the complexity of talent management and the need for organisations to decide whether to focus on identifying high performers and high potentials and adopting consistent or flexible approaches.

Key chapter take-aways

- Talent meanings inform and shape talent identification with dominant meanings embedded in talent management systems and frameworks.
- Talent identification seeks to identify specific individuals who are of greater value than others.
- Talent identification is a judgment-oriented activity by which employees are evaluated compared to, and relative to their peers.
- Talent identification and performance management are not synonymous.

Talent identification: where talent meanings come to life

It is important to start our discussions with a reminder of what talent is. Talent, as illustrated in Chapter 3, is a socially and discursively constructed concept and an idea through which we organise our thoughts. Although talent concepts exist in our minds, perceptions and frames about what talent means (definitions and conceptualisations) at the internalised, individual, interpersonal and localised levels will shape and influence the criteria used to judge and evaluate the workforce. Formalised talent management systems and practices capture and further reinforce dominant meanings as stakeholders are encouraged and incentivised to act in specific ways.

Talent identification is one such crucial practice as stakeholders deploy individual frames when evaluating the workforce according to the defining characteristics of talent, whether that means individuals, skills and capabilities, designated jobs, roles or positions. Regardless of specific talent meanings, talent identification focuses on determining the value of individuals. Talent identification is:

the processes of workforce differentiation which is a judgment-orientated activity whereby we make judgments to determine which individuals are of value, or greater value. Evaluative judgments underpin resource allocations.

Following on from this definition, we identify several key strands underpinning talent identification:

- Its focus is on existing employees of an organisation (Mäkelä, Björkman & Ehrnrooth, 2010).
- It is premised on the view, assumption, perspective and judgment that not all individuals within a workforce are of equal value.
- It seeks to identify a specific pool of employees who are at the 'top' in respect to their performance and capability (Stahl et al., 2007), or a collection of employees with a specific set of characteristics (Jooss et al., 2019a; Tansley & Tietze, 2013).
- Its key aim is to retain, motivate and increase the commitment amongst key individuals via a process of workforce differentiation (Sumelius, Smale & Yamao, 2020).
- It involves a process whereby relevant stakeholders consciously, or unconsciously, partake in comparative judgments of employees.
- It reflects the processes through which talent pools come into being.
- It represents the foundation for decisions about staffing, investments in training and development, and compensation and rewards (Mäkelä et al., 2010).

Talent identification and performance management are not synonymous. While performance ratings generate data used for corporate decision-making on whom to include in talent pools (Cascio, 2006; Stahl et al., 2007) and to varying degrees inform talent identification, evaluations of direct line managers (think about annual performance management processes) are often combined with additional data from wider stakeholders when undertaking talent status determinations (Jooss, Burbach et al., 2019a; Mäkelä et al., 2010; Wiblen, Dery & Grant, 2012). Relevant stakeholders use off-line cognition-based data to make strategic choices when determining which option – in this case, which individuals – are the organisation's talent (Gavetti, 2005; Gavetti & Levinthal, 2000). Gavetti (2005) notes that the position/location of a stakeholder within the organisational hierarchy can influence choice accuracy and managerial decision-making. The ability to evaluate the action-outcome relationships potentially blur when managers progress up the hierarchy and are asked to interpret multiple, heterogeneous domains. These assertions suggest that more senior managers may be less effective in choosing who is talent because they tend to understand and judge more novel actions less favourably than those actions and outcomes which adhere to longitudinal norms and perceptions of an organisation's strategic needs. The ability to conduct talent identification as a two-stage process may help overcome the cognitive limitations of a single individual.

Reviewing many data points from a group of individuals in determining the anticipated and future potential of any specific individual (Mäkelä et al., 2010) permits the inclusion of a multiplicity of perspectives. However, one must be cautious about the extent to which clear decision criteria are in place for talent pool identification purposes. For example, Jooss et al.'s (2019a) examination of talent pool formation in the hospitality industry provides evidence of the disconnect between the rhetoric and reality of talent identification. Analysis of insights derived from 73 in-depth interviews with HR and operational leaders at corporate and business unit levels of three hospitality industry multinational companies (MNCs) found that criteria for talent pool inclusion was notably absent: "it is evident that all MNC's in this research lack clarity in expressing their criteria for inclusion in a TP [talent pool]" (p. 16). The authors also found notable differences between corporate and business unit perspectives. Notwithstanding the absence of clear criteria for inclusion, each MNC did group employees into a multiplicity of talent pools. Given the findings, the authors encourage organisations to develop strategies and frameworks for the various stages of talent identification and ensure that business units are held accountable for practices within their localised contexts to facilitate a more integrated corporate approach.

Talent identification approaches

Literature about talent identification presents an array of normative and prescriptive assumptions about the most effective identification practices, with advocates debating the value of intuitive, individualised and strategic approaches (Bassi & McMurrer, 2007; Jones, Whitaker, Seet & Parkin, 2012). In addition to outlining these discussions to illustrate how researchers propose organisations could or should devise internal talent pools, the following subsections also profile those studies which examine how organisations seek to identify talent.

Talent identification as intuitive and ad hoc practices

The first approach involves the identification of talented employees via processes that are unstructured and informal. Talent determinations derive from the intuitive or 'gut-feel' opinions of specific managers undertaking the evaluation. The intuitive approach is, unsurprisingly, heavily criticised as it speaks to many concerns made about unstructured and ill-considered recruitment and selection practices. Employing an industrial psychology lens, Highhouse (2008) argues that the notion of intuitive experience, whereby HR professionals and other key stakeholders can predict human behaviour and an employee's likelihood of success is a myth. Similarly, Dries (2013) notes that processes underpinned by conjectural assumptions or without formal assessment policies are likely to overestimate the validity of intuitive judgments and may lead to a 'similar-to-me' bias (i.e. a preference for employees more similar to oneself). This scenario would likely raise significant concerns over the diversity of talent pools, with clones of existing talents always more likely. Talent identification through such processes is therefore deemed of little strategic value to organisations because identifying talent based on "instinct and intuition [is] not only inadequate but reckless" (Bassi & McMurrer, 2007, p. 9).

Talent identification as an individualistic approach

Jones et al. (2012) offer two distinct and competing approaches to talent management: an individual or systems-level/strategic focus. The individualistic approach focuses on single individuals who may be 'stars' or employees who possess specific valuable tactical and/or operational skills. Talent identification processes do not include formal assessment policies nor an understanding of the defining characteristics. This approach essentially views talent as a form of human capital and focuses on specific individuals without consideration of contextual factors (Iles, Chuai & Preece, 2010; Jones et al., 2012; McDonnell, 2011). Without an appreciation for team and organisational factors, Beechler and Woodward (2009) argue that the individualistic approach is potentially detrimental rather than beneficial to organisational performance, a point also made by Pfeffer (2001). HR practitioners are often positioned as advocates of individualistic processes because they believe that specific employees possess an 'X factor' or the 'right stuff' (Dries, 2013), and therefore more analytical approaches, based upon metrics or formal evaluations, are unnecessary.

Talent identification as a systematic approach

The vast majority of talent management publications and scholars advocate for the enactment of a strategic and systems approach founded upon the prescriptive assumption that effective talent identification processes are systematic, integrated and proactive (Berger & Berger, 2003; Collings, McDonnell & Scullion, 2009; Collings & Mellahi, 2009; Jooss et al., 2019a; Mellahi & Collings, 2010). Collings and Mellahi (2009, p. 304) suggest that the critical foundation for a strategic talent management system is the "systematic identification" of critical roles within an organisation. Iles et al. (2010) and Stainton (2005) posit that all individuals should go through the same talent identification process. An essential component of talent management, therefore, appears to be the enactment of systematic and consistent talent identification practices (Busine & Watt, 2005). The promulgation of consistent processes can:

- decrease potential personal biases (Dries, 2013) of the senior executive undertaking the evaluation processes.
- minimise reliance on intuition and subjectivity (Highhouse, 2008).
- support procedural and distributive justice (Gelens, Hofmans, Dries & Pepermans, 2014; Greenberg, 2002; O'Connor & Crowley-Henry, 2019) and enable a greater degree of perceived fairness in the evaluation of an employee's performance and/or potential.

Transitioning from 'individualistic' to 'systems' approaches encourages organisations to shift the emphasis away from a sole focus on micro- and individual level talent practices to a macro focus on systems-level issues (Jones et al., 2012). It also encourages organisations to integrate and connect their talent management practices with those of the rest of the organisation (van Dijk, 2008; Whelan & Carcary, 2011; Williamson, 2011). A set of management practices informed by, and aligned to, an organisation's business strategy and enacted systematically is arguably core to talent management. Adoption of a systematic approach would appear to include an emphasis on building talent pipelines and establishing processes to identify and assess high-potential talent. Despite persuasive rhetoric encouraging organisations to connect practices to strategy explicitly, Jones et al.'s (2012) study noted an absence of systematic approaches; rather, describing approaches as ad hoc, unstructured, very fragmented, not uniform and in their infancy.

Implicit in prescriptive instructions about systematic approaches is the implementation and appropriation of a talent management system facilitated through information technology. Technologies such as electronic HRM have the potential to enhance the organisation's ability to efficiently and effectively manage its people-based resources (Farndale, Paauwe & Hoeksema, 2009; Ruël, Bondarouk & Looise, 2004; Schalk, Timmerman & den Heuvel, 2013; Stone & Dulebohn, 2013). Such functionality is of importance to the conduct of transformational activities such as talent management (Parry & Tyson, 2011; Thite & Kavanagh, 2009). Rhetoric asserting that "great systems are often more important than great people" (Beechler & Woodward, 2009, p. 277) further reinforce the value of systematic, consistent and standardised talent identification approaches. Arguably, without appropriate information technology support, a systematic approach to talent management will be challenging for most medium- to large-sized organisations (see Burbach & Royle, 2010; Wiblen, 2016, 2019;

Wiblen, Grant & Dery, 2010; Wiblen & Marler, 2019; Williams, 2009 for insights about the interrelationship between talent management and information technology).

Wiblen et al. (2012) investigated the role of information technology in identifying talent within different business units embedded within the context of a professional services firm. Employing a social construction of technology (SCOT) theoretical perspective, the authors found that the use and the perceived role of technology in helping to identify talent varied. The study found that while some HR managers and business units elected to identify talent with the help of technology to promote consistent, objective and accurate decisions based on data and metrics, the majority of HR and business unit managers sought to identify talent based on subjective evaluations facilitated through conversations and observations. The ability to discuss and debate talent promoted inclusion of multiple perspectives about an individual's performance and potential, thus minimising the propensity to generate talent clones or adopt a one-size-fits-all approach. The findings also highlighted the role of perceptions in shaping talent identification practices. There was evidence of technology-enabled practices emphasising consistency in contexts where metrics were central to business processes and part of everyday discourses and conversations.

Talent identification as evidence and analytics-based approaches

New technologies can enhance decision-making about talent by providing stakeholders, other than just HR professionals, with access to data (Hendrickson, 2003; Pilbeam & Corbridge, 2006; Schalk et al., 2013; Williams, 2009) and hence 'facts' about transactions that occur in organisations daily (Marler & Floyd, 2014). This enables what Rousseau and Barends (2011) refer to as evidence-based decisions which help "HR practitioners develop greater objectivity and balance in their decisions" (p. 233).

The drive to manage talent more effectively has contributed to an increased emphasis placed on talent metrics, with several publications declaring the need for talent decisions to be informed by metrics, data and analytics. Two influential advocates of this approach are Boudreau and Ramstad, who coined the term 'Decision Science' or 'Talentship' where they posit that data will provide a logical, reliable and consistent but flexible framework to enhance decisions about a critical organisational resource (Boudreau & Ramstad, 2002; Boudreau, Ramstad & Dowling, 2002). Bassi and McMurrer (2007) and Williams (2009) express similar sentiments and profess the value of technology in talent management because it affords the capabilities to generate data, information and knowledge about talent, which is vital for achieving a competitive advantage. Indeed, for talent management to be effective, its value and contribution to the organisation's bottom line must be more identifiable (Jones et al., 2012; McDonnell, 2011).

Wiblen (2016) employed discourse analysis as the theoretical and methodological framework to examine how various groups of stakeholders talked about and framed the talent concept within the context of talent identification. Focusing on the talk about talent within specific business unit contexts, the author found evidence of two distinct, if not interrelated, discourses: a measuring and an observing discourse. The measuring discourse asserts that talent is a measurable and quantifiable construct with business units seeking to measure employee performance and prioritise workforce differentiation through a formal ranking process. It advocates for the application of predetermined criteria to evaluate performance to pursue systematic and consistent talent identification processes underpinned by objective metrics. The observing discourse, in contrast, prioritised subjective observations rather than metrics. Rather than infer that numbers, measures and metrics capture specific individuals' value, advocates of the observational perspective focused attention on ensuring talent identification processes were flexible and tailorable to the needs of respective business units at any time. The notion that stakeholders can see and observe one's talent in action was core to this perspective, with human agency key to decision-making and talent status determinations.

Talent identification tensions and decision points

Talent management, when framed as a complex judgment-oriented activity involving resource allocation decisions founded upon perceptions of value, contributes to the complexity of talent identification. Organisations, in effecting decisions about the 'what' (the criteria) and the 'how' (the process) of identifying the 'who' (the specific individuals or groups of individuals) must manage tensions and key decision points.

Focus on performance, potential or both?

Given the domination of the 'individuals as talent' conceptualisation outlined in Chapter 3, the majority of publications assert that organisations should seek to identify specific individuals who achieve higher levels of performance and/or potential when compared relative to their peers. Acknowledging notions of relativity is essential when talking about performance and potential because "talent is not absolute, it is relative and subjective" (Thunnissen, Boselie & Fruytier, 2013, p. 1751). Thus, ideals of high performance and high potential are socially constructed and defined within a specific context and between groups of individuals (both past and present workforces).

While the emphasis on evaluating an individual's strategic value within the performance/potential domain is omnipresent in talent management discourses, organisations must decide whether to focus on an individual's performance, potential, or some combination of both. The latter perspective may prevail in many organisations underpinned by the implementation and enactment of the nine-box matrix which evaluates and ranks individuals according to predefined criteria and an embedded algorithm (more on the role of technology, digitalisation and automation can be found in Chapter 7). The (automatic) identification of talent is often the result of the formulated combination of performance and potential, or at least the belief that both are considered distinctly. In this regard, Jooss, McDonnell and Burbach (2019a) note, in their case study research, a strong conflation between both concepts with limited clarity over measuring potential.

Matters associated with the effectiveness of some combination of performance and potential approach heighten in complexity when reflecting on the elusive nature of potential. Publications seeking to articulate determination criteria include Silzer and Church (2009) who offer a three-dimension model for evaluating it:

- *foundation dimensions* which are stable characteristics associated with personality and cognition.
- *growth dimensions* which are related to the ability and motivation to learn and improve.
- *career dimensions* which incorporate leadership ability, performance rewards and knowledge and value.

Karaevli and Hall (2003) also emphasise an individual's ability and capacity for learning and continuous improvement. Given this is an exercise in forecasting, there is a danger that considerations of potential may amount to little more than crystal ball gazing. Ready, Conger and Hill (2010) similarly seek to demystify the notion of high potential and propose such talented subjects represent 3–5 per cent of an organisation's workforce who have the "X factor" attributed to four intangible factors: a drive to excel, a catalytic learning capability, an enterprising spirit and dynamic sensors that detect opportunities and obstacles.

The concept of potential appears especially critical in views around the 'how' of talent identification because it requires a shift from solely concentrating on the inputs an individual possesses to considering the outputs (Huselid, Beatty & Becker, 2005), and in particular the probability of these outputs. Given this, questions have been raised about the challenges associated with articulating and evaluating potential. Reservations are notably acknowledged by Mellahi and Collings (2010), who, despite positioning themselves as advocates of a systematic approach, "contend that this line of thinking can be misleading when applied to manage talented people. Talent is often tacit, inherently complex and difficult to measure because it often deals with potential rather than performance" (p. 147). Attempting to judge individuals and forecast the possibility and probability of future outputs may be indicative of irresponsible talent management where decisions about resource allocations are informed by little more than an evaluator's gut instinct.

Adopting a consistent or flexible approach

Organisations are required to identify the individuals afforded access to development and retention practices. Debates rage, however, as to whether the systematic (aka consistent) approaches proposed by Collings and Mellahi (2009) are most effective. Talent management systems are valuable because theoretically the value-based criteria on which to judge employees should be defined and individuals privy to a consistent process (Iles et al., 2010; Stainton, 2005), thus creating greater transparency in the 'what' and the 'how' of workforce differentiation. Consistency through standardisation may also permit the transferability of talent identification processes within MNCs (Schmidt, Mansson & Dolles, 2013).

Consistent processes, however, may limit perceptions of talent, resulting in the identification of 'clones' of what organisations already have (McDonnell, 2011) or the ability to recognise idiosyncrasy and diversity (Highhouse, 2008; Mäkelä et al., 2010). Ready et al. (2010, p. 7) specifically encourage CEOs and HR professionals to "be creative" in approaching high-potential talent identification: "That marketing manager from Shanghai who doesn't quite fit your mould might just be the talent you need to win in the future".

A more nuanced understanding and the enactment of practices which possess dexterity and fluidity may enable organisations to react to changes in market conditions and external factors. Flexibility, rather than consistency, may be essential in the current VUCA (volatile, uncertain, complex and ambiguous) environment. However, the reality of what is needed is likely to be the challenging mix and balance of being consistent while also remaining flexible.

Conclusions

The talk about talent identification assumes that grouping specific individuals into talent pools via identification processes is beneficial for employees and organisations (Björkman, Ehrnrooth, Mäkelä, Smale &

Sumelius, 2013; Collings & Mellahi, 2009; Gelens et al., 2014; Sonnenberg, van Zijderveld & Brinks, 2014). Given the agreed value of talent identification, numerous publications (see Table 4.1) focus attention on how organisations could, should and do identify talented subjects who are of higher value, allocate talent status and form internal talent pools. This chapter shows that talent identification could take many forms, including an ad hoc manner underpinned by the intuition of the evaluator; informal processes which focus on specific individuals with the intangible 'X factor'; systematic approaches (commonly facilitated via technology) whereby all individuals are privy to the same processes; occur through analytics and evidence-based approaches. Empirical studies, however, indicate that many organisations elect to identify talent subjects through a two-stage process; in an individualised rather than systematic manner; in a subjective rather than objective way; underpinned by assumptions of whether they 'know talent when they see it'

Table 4.1 Key papers discussing talent identification

Source	Key contribution
Wolfe, Wright and Smart (2006)	The story of MoneyBall focusing on the practical application of the measuring, metrics and evidence-based approach to identifying (sporting) talent.
Boudreau and Ramstad (2005) Boudreau and Ramstad (2006) Boudreau and Ramstad (2007)	Introduces notions of Talentship and a decision science for talent-based decisions. Presents ideas which precede broader discourses about evidence and analytics-based approaches.
Highhouse (2008)	Highlights the complexity of making decisions about an individual's value and their ability to perform, mentioning that humans have an inherent resistance to analytical approaches to selection (with potential transferability of the same assumptions and preferences when selecting internal talent).
Mäkelä et al. (2010)	Examines the decision processes in the identification of internal talent within the MNC context.
Wiblen (2016)	Illustrates that perceptions about whether talent is an observable or measurable construct influence both the extent to which talent decisions are enacted via information technology and how different approaches can occur within the context of a single organisation.

or that an individual's value is best captured via measurable approaches and the allocation of talent scores and ranking processes (again commonly via a technology-enabled algorithm); and without clear talent pool inclusion criteria (see Asplund, 2020; Highhouse, 2008; Jones et al., 2012; Jooss et al., 2019b; Mäkelä et al., 2010; Wiblen, 2016; Wiblen et al., 2012). Furthermore, debates about whether to tell or not tell individuals of their talent status will continue in organisations for years to come. However, researchers would benefit from acknowledging the tension between actions and expectations because, as Sumelius et al. (2020) usefully articulate "employee perceptions of practices rather than the practices themselves are more likely to influence employee attitudes and behaviour" (2020, p. 514). Expectation alignment and perceptions of talent status (Gelens et al., 2014) and the implied 'talent deal' (King, 2016) can potentially influence the effectiveness of talent identification.

Talent identification determinations and the allocation of talent status are influenced by perceptions of the best criteria and processes at numerous levels both within and between organisational boundaries, and it's a wider examination of the nuances of talent identification that will help illuminate the complexity of articulating through frameworks what is (and is not) talent and providing relevant stakeholders with deliberate and strategically aligned frameworks for judging value.

References

Asplund, K. (2020). When profession trumps potential: The moderating role of professional identification in employees' reactions to talent management, *The International Journal of Human Resource Management*, 31: 539–561.

Bassi, L. & McMurrer, D. (2007). Maximising your return on people, *Harvard Business Review*, March: 1–10.

Beechler, S. & Woodward, I. C. (2009). The global "war for talent", *Journal of International Management*, 15: 273–285.

Berger, L. & Berger, D. (Eds.). (2003). *The Talent Management Handbook: Creating a Sustainable Competitive Advantage by Selecting, Developing and Promoting the Best People*, New York: McGraw-Hill Professional.

Björkman, I., Ehrnrooth, M., Mäkelä, K., Smale, A. & Sumelius, J. (2013). Talent or not? Employee reactions to talent identification, *Human Resource Management*, 52: 195–214.

Boudreau, J. W. & Ramstad, P. M. (2002). *Strategic HRM Measurement in the 21st Century: From Justifying HR to Strategic Talent Leadership (CAHRS Working Paper 02–15)*. Retrieved from: https://digitalcommons.ilr.cornell.edu/cgi/viewcontent.cgi?article=1055&context=cahrswp

Boudreau, J. W. & Ramstad, P. M. (2005). Talentship and the new paradigm for human resource management: From professional practices to strategic talent decision science, *Human Resource Planning*, 28: 17–26.

Boudreau, J. W. & Ramstad, P. M. (2006). Talentship and HR measurement and analysis: From ROI to strategic organizational change, *Human Resource Planning*, 29: 25–33.

Boudreau, J. W. & Ramstad, P. M. (2007). *Beyond HR: The New Science of Human Capital*, Boston, MA: Harvard Business School Press.

Boudreau, J. W., Ramstad, P. M. & Dowling, P. J. (2002). *Global Talentship: Towards a Decision Science Connecting Talent to Global Strategic Success (CAHRS Working Paper 02–21)*. Retrieved from: http://digitalcommons.ilr.cornell.edu/cahrswp/62/

Burbach, R. & Royle, T. (2010). Talent on demand?: Talent management in the German and Irish subsidiaries of a US multinational corporation, *Personnel Review*, 39: 414–431.

Busine, M. & Watt, B. (2005). Succession management: Trends and current practice, *Asia Pacific Journal of Human Resources*, 43: 225–237.

Cascio, W. (2006). Global performance management systems, in G. Stahl & I. Björkman (Eds.), *Handbook of Research in International Human Resource Management*, Cheltenham: Edward Elgar, pp. 176–196.

Collings, D. G., McDonnell, A. & Scullion, H. (2009). Global talent management: The law of the few, *Poznan University of Economics Review*, 9: 5–18.

Collings, D. G. & Mellahi, K. (2009). Strategic talent management: A review and research agenda, *Human Resource Management Review*, 19: 304–313.

Dries, N. (2013). The psychology of talent management: A review and research agenda, *Human Resource Management Review*, 23: 272–285.

Farndale, E., Paauwe, J. & Hoeksema, L. (2009). In-sourcing HR: Shared service centres in the Netherlands, *International Journal of Human Resource Management*, 20: 544–561.

Gavetti, G. (2005). Cognition and hierarchy: Rethinking the microfoundations of capabilities' development, *Organization Science*, 16: 599–617.

Gavetti, G. & Levinthal, D. (2000). Looking forward and looking backward: Cognitive and experiential search, *Administrative Science Quarterly*, 45: 113–137.

Gelens, J., Hofmans, J., Dries, N. & Pepermans, R. (2014). Talent management and organisational justice: Employee reactions to high potential identification, *Human Resource Management Journal*, 24: 159–175.

Greenberg, J. (2002). *The Quest for Justice on the Job: Essays and Experiments*, Thousand Oaks, CA: Sage Publications.

Hartmann, E., Feisel, E. & Schober, H. (2010). Talent management of western MNCs in China: Balancing global integration and local responsiveness, *Journal of World Business*, 45: 169–178.

Hendrickson, A. R. (2003). Human resource information systems: Backbone technology of contemporary human resources, *Journal of Labor Research*, 24: 381–394.

Highhouse, S. (2008). Stubborn reliance on intuition and subjectivity in employee selection, *Industrial and Organisational Psychology*, 1: 333–342.

Huselid, M. A., Beatty, R. W. & Becker, B. E. (2005). "A players" or "A positions"? The strategic logic of workforce management, *Harvard Business Review*, December: 110–117.

Iles, P., Chuai, X. & Preece, D. (2010). Talent management and HRM in multinational companies in Beijing: Definitions, differences and drivers, *Journal of World Business*, 45: 179–189.

Jones, J. T., Whitaker, M., Seet, P.-S. & Parkin, J. (2012). Talent management in practice. in Australia: Individualistic or strategic? An exploratory study, *Asia Pacific Journal of Human Resources*, 50: 399–420.

Jooss, S., Burbach, R. & Ruël, H. (2019a). Examining talent pools as a core talent management practice in multinational corporations, *The International Journal of Human Resource Management*, 1–32. https://doi.org/10.1080/09585192.2019.1579748

Jooss, S., McDonnell, A. & Burbach, R. (2019b). Talent designation in practice: An equation of high potential, performance and mobility, *The International Journal of Human Resource Management*, https://doi.org/10.1080/09585192.2019.1686651

Karaevli, A. & Hall, D. T. (2003). Growing leaders for turbulent times: Is succession planning up to the challenge? *Organizational Dynamics*, 32: 62–79.

King, K. A. (2016). The talent deal and journey, *Employee Relations*, 38: 94–111.

Mäkelä, K., Björkman, I. & Ehrnrooth, M. (2010). How do MNCs establish their talent pools? Influences on individuals' likelihood of being labeled as talent, *Journal of World Business*, 45: 134–142.

Marler, J. H. & Floyd, B. D. (2014). Database concepts and applications in human resource information systems, in M. J. Kavanagh, M. Thite & R. D. Johnson (Eds.), *Human Resource Information Systems: Basics, Applications, and Future Directions*, Third edition. Thousand Oaks, CA: SAGE Publications, pp. 34–56.

McDonnell, A. (2011). Still fighting the war for talent? Bridging the science versus practice gap, *Journal of Business and Psychology*, 26: 169–173.

Mellahi, K. & Collings, D. G. (2010). The barriers to effective global talent management: The example of corporate élites in MNEs, *Journal of World Business*, 45: 143–149.

O'Connor, E. P. & Crowley-Henry, M. (2019). Exploring the relationship between exclusive talent management, perceived organisational justice and employee engagement: Bridging the literature, *Journal of Business Ethics*, 156: 903–917.

Parry, E. & Tyson, S. (2011). Desired goals and actual outcomes of e-HRM, *Human Resource Management Journal*, 21: 335–354.

Pfeffer, J. (2001). Fighting the war for talent is hazardous to your organisation's health, *Organizational Dynamics*, 29: 248–259.

Pilbeam, S. & Corbridge, M. (2006). HR information systems and e-enabled HR, in S. Pilbeam & M. Corbridge (Eds.), *People Resourcing: Contemporary HRM in Practice*, Third edition. Harlow: Pearson Education Limited, pp. 121–140.

Ready, D., Conger, J. & Hill, L. (2010). Are you a high potential? *Harvard Business Review*, June.

Rousseau, D. M. & Barends, E. G. R. (2011). Becoming an evidence-based HR practitioner, *Human Resource Management Journal*, 21: 221–235.

Ruël, H., Bondarouk, T. & Looise, J. (2004). E-HRM: Innovation or irritation. An explorative empirical study in five large companies on web-based HRM, *Management Revue*, 15: 364–380.

Schalk, R., Timmerman, V. & den Heuvel, S. V. (2013). How strategic considerations influence decision making on e-HRM applications, *Human Resource Management Review*, 23: 84–92.

Schmidt, C., Mansson, S. & Dolles, H. (2013). Managing talents for global leadership positions in MNCs: Responding to the challenges in China, *Asian Business &
Management*, 12: 477–496.

Silzer, R. & Church, A. H. (2009). The pearls and perils of identifying potential,
Industrial and Organisational Psychology, 2: 377–412.

Sonnenberg, M., van Zijderveld, V. & Brinks, M. (2014). The role of talent-perception
incongruence in effective talent management, *Journal of World Business*, 49: 272–280.

Stahl, G., Björkman, I., Farndale, E., Morris, S. S., Paauwe, J., Stiles, P. & Wright,
P. M. (2007). Global talent management: How leading multinationals build and
sustain their talent pipeline, *INSEAD Working Papers Collection*, 34: 1–36.

Stainton, A. (2005). Talent management: Latest buzzword or refocusing existing
processes? *Competency and Emotional Intelligence*, 12: 39–43.

Stone, D. L. & Dulebohn, J. H. (2013). Emerging issues in theory and research on
electronic human resource management (eHRM), *Human Resource Management
Review*, 23: 1–5.

Sumelius, J., Smale, A. & Yamao, S. (2020). Mixed signals: Employee reactions to
talent status communication amidst strategic ambiguity, *The International Journal of Human Resource Management*, 31: 511–538.

Tansley, C. & Tietze, S. (2013). Rites of passage through talent management progression stages: An identity work perspective, *The International Journal of Human
Resource Management*, 24: 1799–1815.

Thite, M. & Kavanagh, M. J. (2009). Evolution of human resource management and
human resource information systems: The role of information technology, in M.
Thite & M. J. Kavanagh (Eds.), *Human Resource Information Systems. Basics,
Applications, and Future Directions*, Thousand Oaks, CA: SAGE Publications,
pp. 3–24.

Thunnissen, M., Boselie, P. & Fruytier, B. (2013). A review of talent management:
"Infancy or adolescence?", *The International Journal of Human Resource Management*, 24: 1744–1761.

van Dijk, H. G. (2008). The talent management approach to human resource management: Attracting and retaining the right people, *Journal of Public Administration*, 43: 385–395.

Whelan, E. & Carcary, M. (2011). Integrating talent and knowledge management:
Where are the benefits? *Journal of Knowledge Management*, 15: 675–687.

Wiblen, S. (2016). Framing the usefulness of eHRM in talent management: A case
study of talent identification in a professional services firm, *Canadian Journal of
Administrative Sciences*, 33: 95–107.

Wiblen, S. (2019). e-Talent in talent management, in M. Thite (Ed.), *e-HRM: Digital
Approaches, Directions and Applications*, Milton Park: Routledge, pp. 153–171.

Wiblen, S., Dery, K. & Grant, D. (2012). Do you see what I see? The role of technology in talent identification, *Asia Pacific Journal of Human Resources*, 50:
421–438.

Wiblen, S., Grant, D. & Dery, K. (2010). Transitioning to a new HRIS: The reshaping of human resources and information technology talent, *Journal of Electronic Commerce Research*, 11: 251–267.

Wiblen, S. & Marler, J. H. (2019). The human – Technology interface in talent management and the implications for HRM, in R. Bissola & B. Imperatori (Eds.), *HRM 4.0 for Human-Centered Organisations*, Bingley, UK: Emerald Publishing Limited, pp. 99–116.

Williams, H. (2009). Job analysis and HR planning, in M. Thite & M. J. Kavanagh (Eds.), *Human Resource Information Systems: Basics, Applications, and Future Directions*, Thousand Oaks, CA: SAGE Publications, pp. 251–276.

Williamson, D. (2011). Talent management in the new business world: How organisations can create the future and not be consumed by it, *Human Resource Management International Digest*, 19: 33–36.

Wolfe, R., Wright, P. M. & Smart, D. L. (2006). Radical HRM innovation and competitive advantage: The *Moneyball* story, *Human Resource Management*, 45: 111–126.

5 Talent development

Enhancing the value of talented individuals, talent pools or a combination of both

Introduction

There is an unambiguous relationship between talent management and talent development. Researchers agree that talent development is an integral part of a comprehensive talent management system (see Table 2.1 in Chapter 2). Garavan, Carbery and Rock's (2012) review found that talent development publications primarily focus on who is the talent to be developed, what competencies should be developed, who drives development, what is the appropriate pace of development and what is the architecture to support the development. Concerning who should be identified as organisational talent, previous studies provide important insights into whether organisations should adopt exclusive or inclusive approaches (Gallardo-Gallardo, Dries & González-Cruz, 2013; Iles, Chuai & Preece, 2010; Lewis & Heckman, 2006; Stahl et al., 2012; Thunnissen, 2016); the extent to which organisations should prioritise the development of generic or technical skills and/ or competencies (Claussen, Grohsjean, Luger & Probst, 2014; Garavan, Hogan & Cahir-O'Donnell, 2009; Sandberg, 2000; Siikaniemi, 2012); and the popularisation of the 70:20:10 strategy, whereby 70 per cent of talent development takes place through work activities, 20 per cent through relationships and 10 per cent through formal development activities (Wilson, Van Velsor, Chandrasekar & Criswell, 2011).

The chapter shines a light on talent development discussions and debates through an examination of existing research and subsequent evaluation of the core themes in the study and practice of talent development. The chapter begins by framing talent development as a strategic, exclusive and contextually specific activity whereby organisations are encouraged to disproportionately allocate resources to support their strategic goals. We profile the few definitions of talent development before giving an overview of the 'what' of talent development within the broader context of resource allocations. The chapter profiles the handful of studies which examine talent development before highlighting how extant literature reviews tend to refer to development in somewhat insignificant and shallow ways. We also remind readers of the importance of examining talent development as a specific talent management practice. An informed understanding of how organisations develop specific individuals and talent pools can generate insights which potentially generate knowledge about the material differences between talent development and traditional notions of learning and development.

Key chapter take-aways

* Talent development is a strategic practice whereby investments are directed towards activities which will have a greater impact on strategy execution.
* Talent development involves the unequal allocation of resources (e.g. time, attention, access, networking, specific assignments).
* Organisations decide whether to invest in specific individuals, talent pools or a combination of both.
* There is a shortage of talent development studies despite the unanimous agreement that it is an integral part of an organisation's talent management system.

Talent development as a mechanism to pursue strategic goals

Most publications include talent development as part of a broader talent management system in which organisations, regardless of industry, location or size, are encouraged to create and enact policies and processes that endeavour to select, recruit, appraise, identify, engage, motivate and retain valuable talent subjects through processes that are systematic, integrated and proactive (Berger & Berger, 2003; Collings, McDonnell & Scullion, 2009; Collings & Mellahi, 2009; Mellahi & Collings, 2010). Focusing on the building of organisational capability through talent involves the strategic allocation of resources, be it time, attention or monetary, to enhance the capacity of the workforce over time (Day & O'Connor, 2017). Investing in talent development is primarily driven by the organisation's desire to leverage its human talent to deliver results, secure and hold the competitive advantage and attain a strong reputation as an employer, along with being a way to develop individual competencies (Day & O'Connor, 2017). Investments should be connected to the broader organisational strategy (Collings & Mellahi, 2009; Day & O'Connor, 2017; Schmidt, Mansson &

Dolles, 2013; Silzer & Dowell, 2010) of developing talent critical to strategy execution:

> talent management practitioners must carefully diagnose the skills and capabilities required to execute the organisation's strategy and take steps to ensure that those skills and capabilities are available through activities such as selection and talent-pipeline development, through training and development activities, through succession planning, and through thoughtful diagnosis of critical roles and promising talent.
>
> (Cascio, Boudreau & Fink, 2019, p. 67)

We also know that the internal development of organisational talent can enhance industry and firm-specific knowledge and skills (Lepak & Snell, 1999), enable organisations to be competitive (Garavan et al., 2012) and is essential in establishing links between HR and organisational performance (Sheehan, 2012). In sum, talent development should be a key mechanism to realise the frequently purported beneficial outcomes of talent management (as discussed in Chapter 6), increasing employee performance, reducing turnover, reducing absences (Cascio et al., 2019) and establishing or increasing the implied reciprocity of the employment relationship (Asplund, 2020; Björkman, Ehrnrooth, Mäkelä, Smale & Sumelius, 2013; King, 2016; Lehmann, 2009). The impact of development-based activities, however, may be of less value if not intentionally designed to pursue and achieve strategic ambitions and goals.

Talent development as an exclusive activity: focusing on the development of some

Most talent management researchers frame talent development as an exclusive activity (Baum, 2008 is an exception). Through advocation of the unequal allocation of resources, researchers, whether intentionally or inherently, encourage organisations to focus on developing some of the workforce in different ways. Other members of the workforce who do not receive talent status are, however, still supported through more traditional learning and development activities. In other words, while talent development may speak to more significant investment in some, this does not suggest that it should be to the wider neglect of the workforce. Accordingly, we reinforce the call for an appropriately high baseline support of all staff development.

Identified talent subjects – be they referred to as high-potential and/or high-performing employees (Collings & Mellahi, 2009; King, 2016; Stahl et al., 2007; Swailes & Blackburn, 2016) – participate in a wider selection of activities than those not identified as talent. As King (2016, p. 98) notes, organisations apply a talent identification process to identify high-potential employees for future advancement and inclusion in talent programmes. Indeed, the identification of someone as talent is likely to alter the psychological contract (see Chapter 6 for more discussion) where such individuals will expect something extra to others (Sonnenberg, van Zijderveld & Brinks, 2014).

Talent development as a contextually specific activity

Day and O'Connor (2017) usefully acknowledge that the topic of talent development in organisations requires an appreciation of the context in which this takes place. As Day and O'Connor (2017) and Wiblen and McDonnell (2020) highlight, both the meaning of talent and the practice of talent management are contextually embedded. Thus, the processes of talent development will likely differ between organisations. Development plans for talent subjects are also contextual, with HR and/or line managers simultaneously tasked with personalising and customising resource allocations to meet the needs of specific individuals (Barlow, 2006; Day & O'Connor, 2017) and ensure that an individual's increased performance aligns with the needs of the organisation and contributes to strategy execution.

Given the contextually specific nature of talent development, researchers should critically reflect on the effectiveness of structured and consistently applied activities. While these may be more efficient, the need to reflect upon the requirements of each talent subject may be more effective. Moves towards customisation rather than consistency in development may be of greater value to organisations because the different kinds of strategic behaviours, and therefore skills, required will vary (Jensen, Poulfelt & Kraus, 2010; Porter, 1979). Regardless of whether deploying consistent or tailored approaches to talent development, there is little doubt that it represents a practice encased with notions of mutual reciprocity. Both organisations and individuals play an active role in extracting and converting the resources allocated in ways which align with the organisation's strategic needs. While organisations play a role in facilitating talent development, individuals must take charge of their development activities (Barlow, 2006; Baum, 2008; D'Annunzio-Green, 2008) with assertions that responsibility for talent development increasingly resides with individuals.

The attributes worthy of development are also contextually specific. Schmidt et al. (2013) acknowledge the cultural specificity of leadership talent while commenting on developing future leaders of an MNC in its Chinese subsidiary. Drawing on Gerstner and Day (1994), Schmidt et al. (2013, p. 480) remind researchers of the relationship between development and perceptions: "In order to operate effectively as a leader, an individual must first be perceived as a leader by the people he/she is leading (Gerstner & Day, 1994). If the leadership competencies developed by leadership development practices and programs in MNCs are not perceived as leadership competencies by employees in the host country, problematic issues may arise (Gerstner & Day, 1994)". Organisations, therefore, are required to develop internal talent through programmes which acknowledge both national and organisational cultures.

Definitions and perspectives

While most talent management publications reference 'development', specific definitions of talent development are sparse. Lewis and Heckman (2006, p. 140), when discussing talent definitions, acknowledged, albeit indirectly, that organisations can pursue talent development in different ways: where 'talent', a high-performing or high-potential talent is managed to their performance levels; or where organisations manage the performance pools of talent. The authors state that seeking to maximise and manage the "talent inherent in each person" is well intended but not strategic because it provides no underlying framework to allocate resources effectively (Lewis & Heckman, 2006, p. 141). Instead, in advocating for explicit alignment between talent decisions and an organisation's strategic talent direction, Lewis and Heckman (2006) call for informed decisions about which talent category warrants greater investment.

Day and O'Connor (2017) state that "In essence, talent development addresses how to change individuals and collectives in desired ways over time" (p. 343) and that "involves targeted investment in those individuals with the greatest potential to build and deploy capabilities to influence the achievement of strategic organisational objectives significantly and develop the capacity in others to do so" (p. 349). In doing so, these authors encourage organisations to avoid solely focusing on high-level incumbents with avenues to prepare others for the possibility of fulfilling strategic positions also key.

Some writings attempt to draw distinctions between talent development as a focus on individuals and a focus on talent pools. For example, while acknowledging the value of affording additional resources to talent as a means to improve day-to-day job performance, Cascio et al. (2019, pp. 366–367) appeal to HR and talent-based practitioners to also "select the *programs* (emphasis added) that will have the greatest impact on pivotal talent pools – those where investments in HRD will have the largest marginal impact on activities, decisions and ultimately, on the value created for the firm". The emphasis, therefore, should be on devising programmes which seek to increase the value of a pivotal talent pool, rather than a specific talent subject per se.

Talent development, therefore, can focus on:

- Individualistic perspectives whereby investment focuses on further enhancing the talent of specific individuals who have previously been identified.
- Collectivist perspectives whereby investment focuses on developing the talent pool (consisting of individuals identified as talent) comprising specific individuals who are being primed to transition into pivotal roles and (leadership) positions.

In seeking to capture the exclusivity associated with resource allocation, we define talent development as:

> the provision of organisational resources, monetary and non-monetary, to individual talent subjects judged as of greater value to the pursuit and realisation of an organisation's strategic ambitions.
>
> (*Wiblen & Tansley, 2017*).

Resources for allocation

Talent development involves more than just permitting talent access to established learning and development activities. Investing stronger in the development of some, rather than all the workforce, requires organisations and the relevant stakeholders to devise and enact strategically relevant activities. Organisations, therefore, need to determine which activities will garner greater investment returns. There is a multiplicity of perspectives about which resources talent can or should access. Development activities include but are not limited to:

- Rewards and incentives to transfer learning to increase day-to-day job performance (Cascio et al., 2019).
- New, expanded or challenging job assignments (Asplund, 2020; Barnett & Davis, 2008; Cascio et al., 2019) or activities where current capabilities are tested (Day, 2007; McCauley, Van Velsor & Ruderman, 2010).
- Action-learning projects whereby subjects work on organisational problems in real time (Asplund, 2020; Day, 2007).
- Access to internal or external training programmes (Cascio et al., 2019; Sumelius, Smale & Yamao, 2020).

- Job rotations (Day & O'Connor, 2017; Lehmann, 2009; Wang-Cowham, 2011).
- Global job rotations and international assignments or exposure (Day & O'Connor, 2017; Schmidt et al., 2013; Wang-Cowham, 2011).
- Education including access to formal programmes (e.g. MBA or Executive MBA) (Day & O'Connor, 2017; Lehmann, 2009; Wang-Cowham, 2011).
- Assessment such as 360-degree feedback (Day & O'Connor, 2017) to diagnose the current state of the individual in terms of leadership capacity (Day, 2007; McCauley et al., 2010).
- Mentoring (informal or formal) where a senior person invests in the personal and professional development of the individual (Barnett & Davis, 2008; Day, 2007; Day & O'Connor, 2017; Lehmann, 2009).
- Additional coaching and training (Asplund, 2020; Barnett & Davis, 2008).
- Executive coaching including sensemaking of assessment feedback and devising development plans (Day, 2007; Day & O'Connor, 2017).
- Senior leadership and/or line manager support (Day & O'Connor, 2017; McCauley et al., 2010) which can take the form of positive reinforcement from co-workers, bosses and the broader environment to build self-confidence (Day, 2007).
- Access to corporate or external universities (Day, 2007; Wang-Cowham, 2011).
- Accelerated promotion (Day, 2007), prioritisation for new internal promotions (Sumelius et al., 2020) or more career opportunities (Asplund, 2020).
- Exposure to, and networking with, senior executives (Day, 2007; Sumelius et al., 2020).
- Attendance at or participation in professional and/or industry conferences (Day, 2007).
- Favourable treatments (e.g. bonuses, quick advancement) (Meyers, van Woerkom, Paauwe & Dries, 2020).
- Membership to a select talent-based group (Asplund, 2020).
- Ability to apply for certain leadership positions (Asplund, 2020).
- Skill, competency, and behaviour development to contribute to successful careers (Iles et al., 2010; Schmidt et al., 2013).
- Development of cross-cultural leadership skills (Schmidt et al., 2013).

Regardless of the approach, Cascio et al. (2019, p. 364) call on organisations to recognise the need to prepare talent for their forthcoming development: "First, candidates for development must be prepared and motivated to both learn and to apply their learning at work". Preparation is followed by the development 'experience' – such as the job or training programme. These authors usefully acknowledge the salience of the environment in which development is transferred and note that to facilitate the improved performance of the talent, organisations need to provide an environment that provides the opportunity and motivation to apply and transfer their learning. Consequently, talent development, to some extent, focuses as much on facilitating an environment for learning transfer and behaviour changes as much as it is about affording the development experience itself. In effect, no one practice or approach works or fails solely on its own right.

What do the empirical studies tell us? There's only a handful

While many definitions of talent management incorporate development, studies that examine how organisations seek to undertake this practice are notably absent. This is evident from our consideration of the literature and the various review papers (see Table 1.1 in Chapter 1) which illustrate that talent development as a specific practice is rarely featured. Next we provide a brief overview of the handful of studies that exist.

Lehmann (2009) examined knowledge workers employed within Thailand and Malaysia. Qualitative interviews with individuals deriving from various industries found that the development of talented employees included posting their identification, which was deemed essential for the effective management of talent within their respective organisations. The competencies of talents were advanced through individualised training programmes which involved formal education and training, as well as job rotations, coaching and mentoring arrangements that were designed to make individuals assume responsibility for their learning and self-development (p. 161). The paper highlights the contextually specific nature of talent development and argues that the benefits of investing in developing talent can be counterbalanced by social, organisational and managerial contexts as these influence the extent to which proclaimed benefits come to fruition.

Drawing from knowledge-sharing and social exchange theory, Wang-Cowham (2011) explores the connection between talent development and knowledge-sharing mechanisms. Based on the idea that the intentional design and subsequent facilitation of knowledge-sharing opportunities support talent development, the author considers the experiences of Chinese HR managers. Asked to describe their learning journeys, HR managers noted that on-the-job training, studying external degrees, overseas training and exposure, learning desire and social networks shaped learning or updating their knowledge and experiences of working in HRM, thus affording empirical insights into the resources allocated to develop HR professionals.

The study also notes that the deliberate inclusion of knowledge-sharing and socialisation mechanisms can nurture an ideal environment for ideas-testing, skills-practising, knowledge, and best practice sharing whereby talent can apply ideas gained from development activities.

Schmidt et al. (2013) examine the transferability of identification and development practices of Swedish MNCs to their China subsidiaries. The findings highlight challenges associated with transferring development processes of their talent management approach. Issues with mobility featured Chinese respondents framing international assignments and mobility as undesirable. There was little evidence of severe issues overall with very limited local adaptation in development programmes. This study also confirms the tension between standardising and tailoring development activities and programmes with evidence that some, not all MNCs, allow a certain degree of adjustment to developing talent across their global operations. Regardless of the specific MNC, the authors noted that talent development practices at the advanced leadership levels are globally standardised. They conceded that operating at the global level requires future senior leadership talent to adhere to global, rather than nationally specific, standards and requirements. Notwithstanding the usefulness of these empirical insights, it is essential to note that the paper offers no definition of talent development, thus contributing to the ongoing ambiguity noted in Chapters 2 and 3.

Wiblen and Tansley (2017) consider how organisations may differentiate between talent development and more traditional learning and development. The authors employ discourse analysis when examining the two-year talent development programme of a professional services firm. Usefully, this study shows that organisations will invest disproportionately in a talent pool consisting of specific talent subjects to pursue strategic endeavours. In this way, talent development as a strategic activity is about more than learning and development; talent development is about allocating resources – such as access to formal mentorship, formalised training and skill development, exposure to senior leadership and networking – in strategically relevant ways.

Conclusion

While industry practitioners have written about talent development approaches and 'best practices' for many decades (for example see Barlow, 2006), this chapter illustrates that much of the academic discussion is limited and superficial. Specific definitions of talent development are sparse if present at all. Academics agree that talent management includes talent development and that developing talented subjects involves accessing additional resources. We have a long list, however, of the various forms and structures such resources could entail from individual motivation to international secondments, to access to formalised learning and education.

We encourage scholars to enquire about the underlying assumptions about talent when examining talent development phenomena because perceptions about talent – the concept – will influence who is in receipt and how organisations enact talent development. Importantly, debates about whether talent is an innate or acquired attribute (Meyers, van Woerkom & Dries, 2013) feature in discussions about talent development. Academics and practitioners alike will establish talent development policies and programmes which seek to account for and balance numerous tensions, including assertions and assumptions about whether:

- individuals are born with their talents versus talent can be developed (the salient nature-nurture debate).
- individuals should focus on developing their strengths or their weaknesses.
- some individuals are born to be leaders versus the ability to prepare individuals to become leaders whereby we build leadership skills and capabilities.
- talent is a set of accomplishments that results from many years of training versus we can immediately develop a specific skill and capability.

Critical analysis of extant talent management reviews highlights that examination of talent development is notably absent. While these reviews cannot include (i.e. papers) what doesn't exist, the omission of broader discussions about how organisations develop their talent is somewhat perplexing and worthy of reflection given that scholars unanimously agree that talent management includes the development of talented subjects. One reason may be that the ability to decipher boundaries between what is talent development and what is leadership development may be fraught with complexity. Given the emphasis on individual conceptualisations whereby specific individuals, including future leaders, are evaluated as valuable and indicative of talent subjects, combined with the ubiquitous leadership development programmes, may mean that conversations about these two concepts are synonymous. Other reasons could be that leadership is an accepted and established area of study, which means there are accepted theoretical models to apply to assist with the peer-review process, and learning and development are considered part of traditional HRM; therefore, many organisations focus on inclusive approaches to development.

References

Asplund, K. (2020). When profession trumps potential: The moderating role of professional identification in employees' reactions to talent management, *The International Journal of Human Resource Management*, 31: 539–561.

Barlow, L. (2006). Talent development: The new imperative? *Development and Learning in Organisations*, 20: 6–9.

Barnett, R. & Davis, S. (2008). Creating greater success in succession planning, *Advances in Developing Human Resources*, 10: 721–739.

Baum, T. (2008). Implications of hospitality and tourism labour markets for talent management strategies, *International Journal of Contemporary Hospitality Management*, 20: 720–729.

Berger, L. & Berger, D. (Eds.). (2003). *The Talent Management Handbook: Creating a Sustainable Competitive Advantage by Selecting, Developing and Promoting the Best People*, New York: McGraw-Hill Professional.

Björkman, I., Ehrnrooth, M., Mäkelä, K., Smale, A. & Sumelius, J. (2013). Talent or not? Employee reactions to talent identification, *Human Resource Management*, 52: 195–214.

Cascio, W., Boudreau, J. & Fink, A. (2019). *Investing in People: Financial Impact of Human Resource Initiatives*, Third edition. Alexandria, VA: Society for Human Resource Management (SHRM).

Claussen, J., Grohsjean, T., Luger, J. & Probst, G. (2014). Talent management and career development: What it takes to get promoted, *Journal of World Business*, 49: 236–244.

Collings, D. G., McDonnell, A. & Scullion, H. (2009). Global talent management: The law of the few, *Poznan University of Economics Review*, 9: 5–18.

Collings, D. G. & Mellahi, K. (2009). Strategic talent management: A review and research agenda, *Human Resource Management Review*, 19: 304–313.

D'Annunzio-Green, N. (2008). Managing the talent management pipeline: Towards a greater understanding of senior managers' perspectives in the hospitality and tourism sector, *International Journal of Contemporary Hospitality Management*, 20: 807–819.

Day, D. V. (2007). Developing leadership talent: A guide to succession planning and leadership development. *SHRM Foundation's Effective Practice Guidelines Series*. Retrieved from: www.shrm.org/hr-today/trends-and-forecasting/special-reports-and-expert-views/Documents/Developing-Leadership-Talent.pdf

Day, D. V. & O'Connor, P. M. G. (2017). Talent development: Building organizational capability, in D. G. Collings, K. Mellahi & W. F. Cascio (Eds.), *The Oxford Handbook of Talent Management*, Oxford: Oxford University Press, pp. 343–360.

Gallardo-Gallardo, E., Dries, N. & González-Cruz, T. F. (2013). What is the meaning of "talent" in the world of work? *Human Resource Management Review*, 23: 290–300.

Garavan, T. N., Carbery, R. & Rock, A. (2012). Mapping talent development: Definition, scope and architecture, *European Journal of Training and Development*, 36: 5–24.

Garavan, T. N., Hogan, C. & Cahir-O'Donnell, A. (2009). *Developing Managers and Leaders: Perspectives, Debates and Practices in Ireland*, Dublin: Gill Education.

Gerstner, C. R. & Day, D. V. (1994). Cross-cultural comparison of leadership prototypes, *The Leadership Quarterly*, 5: 121–134.

Iles, P., Chuai, X. & Preece, D. (2010). Talent management and HRM in multinational companies in Beijing: Definitions, differences and drivers, *Journal of World Business*, 45: 179–189.

Jensen, S. H., Poulfelt, F. & Kraus, S. (2010). Managerial routines in professional service firms: Transforming knowledge into competitive advantages, *Service Industries Journal*, 30: 2045–2062.

King, K. A. (2016). The talent deal and journey, *Employee Relations*, 38: 94–111.

Lehmann, S. (2009). Motivating talents in Thai and Malaysian service firms, *Human Resource Development International*, 12: 155–169.

Lepak, D. P. & Snell, S. A. (1999). The human resource architecture: Toward a theory of human capital allocation and development, *Academy of Management Review*, 24: 31–48.

Lewis, R. E. & Heckman, R. J. (2006). Talent management: A critical review, *Human Resource Management Review*, 16: 139–154.

McCauley, C. D., Van Velsor, E. & Ruderman, M. N. (2010). Introduction: Our view of leadership development, in E. Van Velsor, C. D. McCauley & M. N. Ruderman (Eds.), *The Center for Creative Leadership Handbook of Leadership Development*, Hoboken: John Wiley & Sons, pp. 1–26.

Mellahi, K. & Collings, D. G. (2010). The barriers to effective global talent management: The example of corporate élites in MNEs, *Journal of World Business*, 45: 143–149.

Meyers, M. C., van Woerkom, M. & Dries, N. (2013). Talent – Innate or acquired? Theoretical considerations and their implications for talent management, *Human Resource Management Review*, 23: 305–321.

Meyers, M. C., van Woerkom, M., Paauwe, J. & Dries, N. (2020). HR managers' talent philosophies: Prevalence and relationships with perceived talent management practices, *The International Journal of Human Resource Management*, 31: 562–588.

Porter, M. E. (1979). The structure within industries and companies' performance, *The Review of Economics and Statistics*, 61: 214–227.

Sandberg, J. (2000). Understanding human competence at work: An interpretative approach, *Academy of Management Journal*, 43: 9–25.

Schmidt, C., Mansson, S. & Dolles, H. (2013). Managing talents for global leadership positions in MNCs: Responding to the challenges in China, *Asian Business & Management*, 12: 477–496.

Sheehan, M. (2012). Developing managerial talent: Exploring the link between management talent and perceived performance in multinational corporations (MNCs), *European Journal of Training and Development*, 36: 66–85.

Siikaniemi, L. (2012). Information pathways for the competence foresight mechanism in talent management framework, *European Journal of Training and Development*, 36: 46–65.

Silzer, R. & Dowell, B. (2010). Strategic talent management matters, in R. Silzer & B. Dowell (Eds.), *Strategy-Driven Talent Management: A Leadership Imperative*, San Francisco: Jossey Bass, pp. 3–72.

Sonnenberg, M., van Zijderveld, V. & Brinks, M. (2014). The role of talent-perception incongruence in effective talent management, *Journal of World Business*, 49: 272–280.

Stahl, G. K., Björkman, I., Farndale, E., Morris, S. S., Paauwe, J., Stiles, P. & Wright, P. M. (2007). Global talent management: How leading multinationals build and sustain their talent pipeline, *INSEAD Working Papers Collection*, 34: 1–36.

Stahl, G. K., Björkman, I., Farndale, E., Morris, S. S., Paauwe, J., Stiles, P. & Wright, P. M. (2012). Six principles of effective global talent management, *MIT Sloan Management Review*, 53: 25–32.

Sumelius, J., Smale, A. & Yamao, S. (2020). Mixed signals: Employee reactions to talent status communication amidst strategic ambiguity, *The International Journal of Human Resource Management*, 31: 511–538.

Swailes, S. & Blackburn, M. (2016). Employee reactions to talent pool membership, *Employee Relations*, 38: 112.

Thunnissen, M. (2016). Talent management: For what, how and how well? An empirical exploration of talent management in practice, *Employee Relations*, 38: 57–72.

Wang-Cowham, C. (2011). Developing talent with an integrated knowledge-sharing mechanism: An exploratory investigation from the Chinese human resource managers' perspective, *Human Resource Development International*, 14: 391–407.

Wiblen, S. & McDonnell, A. (2020). Connecting "talent" meanings and multi-level context: A discursive approach, *The International Journal of Human Resource Management*, 31: 474–510.

Wiblen, S. & Tansley, C. (2017). *Talking about Talent Development in Professional Services: An Australian Case Study.* Paper presented at the Academy of Management Annual Meeting: At the Interface, Atlanta, United States.

Wilson, M. S., Van Velsor, E., Chandrasekar, A. & Criswell, C. (2011). *Grooming Top Leaders: Cultural Perspectives from China, India, Singapore, and the United States*. Retrieved from: www.ccl.org/wp-content/uploads/2011/04/Grooming TopLeaders.pdf

6 The impact of talent management
Unpacking the evidence

Introduction

The exponential growth in talent management research owes much to organisational leaders identifying it as one of their most important business challenges given its cited centrality to competitive advantage (Cappelli & Keller, 2014). However, what do we know about the impact of talent management? Is there evidence that demonstrates the purported positive effects are realised? Is there a negative side to talent management? What boundary conditions may support positive outcomes and/or reduce any negative consequences? We contend that the answers to such questions are amongst those of the most fundamental importance because much of the rise of talent management as a strategic management activity can be traced to perceptions of positive impact.

There has been a debate amongst scholars over recent years on whether talent management is in fact a positive approach to workforce management. On one side there is the argument that, by investing in talent management practices, organisations will gain considerably through stronger job and organisational performance, retention of key individuals and development of stronger talent pipelines whereby a greater pool of the internal labour market can be primed to move into several roles (Collings & Mellahi, 2009; Garavan, 2012). On the other side is a more critical perspective whereby talent management is viewed as further evidence of an overly marketised orientation that too commonly sees capital as the dominant interest over other legitimate interests and is an extreme form of treating people as resources to be used (Dundon & Rafferty, 2018, p. 382). The argument put forward is that talent management belittles many important functions and roles which can lead to more negative effects such as reduced motivation and morale amongst workers and lower productivity (Marchington, 2015; Marescaux, De Winne & Sels, 2013; Swailes, 2013).

We contend that these debates are healthy, especially as it means different disciplinary and philosophical perspectives are being incorporated into the talent management discourse. It can be argued that the incorporation of greater disciplinary plurality to address key research questions in which talent management researchers are interested is likely to serve knowledge and practice greatly. Sparrow and Makram (2015, p. 249) have noted an evident increased diversity in talent management studies representing "different values, assumptions, allegiances and philosophies". This, they argue, leads the field to a critical juncture that needs to be addressed for it to advance; namely, what is the underpinning value of talent management? In this chapter, we consider the existing base of empirical research to shed light on the answer to this question. In so doing, we can see that limited empirical enquiry exists and that results are somewhat mixed. Hence, proclamations of talent management being a force of good needs to be tempered until further evidence is provided.

Key chapter take-aways

- There is limited empirical enquiry on the impact of talent status and talent management practices on outcomes across individual, team and organisational levels.
- Existing evidence is mixed, but both positive and negative impacts have been found on how individuals react to talent management.

Talent management and individual outcomes

The various reviews of the talent management literature have noted that relatively limited attention has been placed on the most central stakeholder (i.e. individual talents) (e.g. McDonnell, Collings, Mellahi & Schuler, 2017). However, some notable exceptions exist which are summarised in Tables 6.1 and 6.2.

The evidence for positive effects from talent status

With regards to the impact of talent status or labels, there is evidence that indicates that the mere perception by individuals of being identified as a talent leads to positive employee attitudes. In effect, there appears to be a buoyancy from being part of the talent pool membership versus those who are not (Swailes & Blackburn, 2016). Björkman, Ehrnrooth, Mäkelä, Smale and Sumelius's (2013) study was the first that analysed the relationship between individuals being labelled as talents and the resultant employee attitudes that were exhibited. They found significant differences between employees who perceived that they had been identified as talent and those who had not been, and also those who were unsure if they were a talent or not in the eyes of the organisation. Where individuals perceived themselves as having talent status, the evidence was that these were more likely to be associated with an increased commitment to increasing performance demands, to building competencies of value for the organisation, lower turnover intentions and identifying with their focal unit. These findings were stable, other than for turnover intention, when compared to those employees who reported that they were unsure of their talent status. These results led Björkman et al. (2013) to suggest that being aware of one's talent status appears to offer a motivational impact. Moreover, the lack of a statistically significant difference between those who were not identified as a talent and those who were unsure intimated that potential negative motivational impacts by non-talents may be limited.

Psychological contract theory is especially useful here to help understand that talent status may alter the expectations of both parties. The line of argument is that having talent status and the opportunities and investment that this may afford may obligate individuals to enhance their work behaviours to deliver more for the firm (Festing & Schäfer, 2014; Höglund, 2012). Therefore, talent status may positively influence the psychological contract of those in receipt of talent status, and this may lead to positive attitudinal, behavioural and performance effects (Björkman et al., 2013). Social exchange theory tends to also be used in studies that consider such matters, with Björkman et al.'s (2013) findings supporting its utility as a theoretical frame (Blau, 1964). The central piece of this theory is that once an organisation invests in individuals, then this will lead to reciprocation through higher levels of discretionary behaviour (Cropanzano & Mitchell, 2005; McClean & Collins, 2011).

Another theoretical lens that appears useful in this regard, but which has received limited attention, is 'identity' (Kirk, 2020; Tansley & Tietze, 2013). In effect, once an individual is named as a talent, it is assigning an 'identity' to that person which in turn will bring new connotations for both the individual and organisation. In effect, it can be argued that assigning someone with a talent label places a particular identity on this person. As a result, expectations will rise to go with this label due to a particular set of meanings that are seen as characteristic of such individuals (Strauss, 2017). Importantly, as we turn to later in this chapter, this identity may not be solely positive.

While the early studies intimated positive employee reactions from being a talent, more recent work suggests that a more complex interaction effect may exist that goes beyond the simple equation:

Talent status = improved employee attitudes and reactions.

Table 6.1 Key empirical papers on outcomes arising from talent status

Reference	Type of study	Key findings
Kirk (2020)	Qualitative	Highlights the tensions that being named as a global talent places on an individual and how this identity can be negotiated and resisted.
Sumelius, Smale and Yamao (2020)	Qualitative	Reveals how contextual effects of strategic ambiguity in the communication of talent status affects the reactions of both those with the talent label and those without.
Ehrnrooth et al. (2018)	Quantitative	Questions the literature that indicates a straightforward and direct relationship exists between talent status awareness and talent attitudes.
Swailes and Blackburn (2016)	Qualitative	Individuals classified as talents were more positive about their future prospects than non-talent pool employees, who also reported higher perceptions of unfairness, lower feelings of being supported by the organisation and the interest in them by their employer.
Seopa, Wocke and Leeds (2015)	Quantitative	Talent status is positively related to a relational psychological contract and higher levels of organisational commitment, but no relationship was established with turnover intentions, and trust does not necessarily translate into trust.
Dries and De Gieter (2014)	Qualitative	Talent status creates expectations amongst the information, and information asymmetry on this can be a substantial risk for psychological contract breach and can lead to the opposite effects on those sought by the organisation.
Gelens, Dries, Hofmans and Pepermans (2013)	Quantitative	Talents and non-talents have different responses to workforce differentiation. Perceptions of procedural and distributive justice influence individual-level outcomes of talent status.
Björkman et al. (2013)	Quantitative	Employees who believe to have been identified as a talent report greater positive attitudinal outcome versus those who are unsure of their talent status or who are not talents.

Sonnenberg, van Zijderveld and Brinks (2014) found that employees who were clear about their talent status had higher psychological contract fulfilment. However, their research indicates that there may be an interactional effect with organisational inducements. Specifically, an individual who incorrectly believes they have been identified as a talent in the organisation is positively related to psychological contract fulfilment, but this correlation becomes negative when talent management practices are controlled for. Similarly, Gelens, Hofmans, Dries and Pepermans (2014) considered the link between individuals classified as a high potential and job satisfaction and work effort. They found that perceived distributive justice mediated the association between being a high potential and the levels of reported job satisfaction. The study also demonstrated that the levels of distributive justice were highest amongst talents. Further, this research discovered that perceptions of procedural justice had a moderating effect on the relationship between perceived distributive justice and work effort. Importantly, Gelens et al. (2014) articulate the importance of subjectivity in that perceptions of both procedural and distributive justice are important in the individual level outcomes arising from the differentiation involved in talent management. This study mitigated methodological limitations like common method variance, as acknowledged by Björkman et al. (2013), using archival data. This enabled stronger conclusions to be drawn on how organisations differentiate between employees and the effects this has.

More recent work by Ehrnrooth et al. (2018) fundamentally "call into question extant research on the direct motivational effect of talent status awareness" (p. 444). This research indicates that talent status awareness moderates the response of talents to organisational inducements which leads to a change in obligations rather than being a simplistic direct relationship. More specifically, it was found that individuals who were aware of their talent status responded in a stronger manner to development practices and had higher psychological contract fulfilment. These findings suggest that awareness of one's talent status makes individuals far more attuned to what they are offered for their inherent value, and that being labelled as a talent may not be sufficient in its own right (Gelens et al., 2014). As a result, talents' attitudes may be shaped by a combination of talent status and focused organisational practices that induce positive reactions. The underpinning idea of much talent management scholarship that talents need to receive disproportionate investment therefore seems relevant.

The negative side of talent status

The sparse literature examining the reactions to talent status has been heavily focused on more positive outcomes. It largely assumes that gaining talent designation is a highly valuable resource (Asplund, 2020). Studies, especially those with quantitative methodologies, have tended to ignore the potentially negative outcomes that may arise from being a talent and 'subject to' talent management. There is some qualitative evidence that points to higher daily stress levels and substantial personal sacrifices (see Tansley & Tietze, 2013). Applying an auto-ethnographic approach, Daubner-Siva, Ybema, Vinkenburg and Beech (2018, p. 75) relate being a talent to a double-edged sword that involves both feelings of power and powerlessness. Kirk (2020) adopted an especially interesting approach that draws on socio-onomastics – the meaning of names – to reveal that those labelled as a global talent reported substantial identity struggles by having to reconcile several tensions (expectation around global travel versus other identities such as husband, wife, dad, mother). The lived experience approach adopted in this study unpacked the dynamic and negotiated nature of identity of talents. Why may there be a real negative angle to those who are deemed as the most important the organisation has and who are likely to receive additional investment and supports? This appears to be linked to feelings of needing to show continuous improvement, having to be highly flexible, being subject to considerable monitoring and a feeling of always having to be at the 'top of your game'. Access to additional opportunities and resources because of one's talent status may invite the attention of peers, which some can consider unwelcome.

Ready, Conger and Hill (2010) explicitly recognise the repositioning of expectations and some challenges: "People's expectations of you are high, and colleagues who aren't on the list may secretly, perhaps unconsciously, want you to falter, or even resent you enough to hope you fall from grace" (p. 7). Some publications frame discretionary performance and improved ties between an individual and the organisation as resulting from disproportionate investment (see Collings & Mellahi, 2009). While outcomes-based rhetoric supports the ideals of talent management and talent development per se, they rarely concede the dark side of inherent assumptions: that these individuals will go 'above and beyond' job requirements, tolerate less-than-ideal working conditions and may sacrifice individual needs for the success of the organisation.

The impact on those not identified or labelled as talented is also one that merits much consideration. There are arguments made that any positive effects that may be realised by those who receive talent status could be eroded by the negative impact on everyone else (Marescaux et al., 2013). In this vein, O'Connor and Crowley-Henry (2019) note a need to "reject that all employees perceive the fairness of TM in the same way" (p. 904). These authors note how some scholars (e.g. Lacey & Groves, 2014) see hypocrisy between the practice of corporate social responsibility and the pursuit of exclusive talent management, where the majority of the workforce is denied access to focused development opportunities. The idea that every organisation has a responsibility to develop and care for all its workforce is one to which we subscribe. Indeed, we suggest that our interpretation of the literature is that few argue differently. Our interpretation is instead that many talent management scholars speak more about talent pools, segmentation and differentiation than about the need for pure elitist approaches whereby those not included in a talent management programme are forgotten about.

Influencing factors on talent status outcomes: transparency and communication

The extent to which positive and/or negative effects occur based on how talents and 'non-talents' react appears to be impacted by several factors (procedural and distributive justice were highlighted earlier in the chapter). Transparency and communication in terms of whether one was classified as a talent or not and the expectations on those with such designations (Dries & De Gieter, 2014; Festing, Kornau & Schäfer, 2015) appear especially relevant. There are studies that argue if organisations want to create positive outcomes from talent management, then it is vital that there is transparent communication on talent status (Sonnenberg et al., 2014). Interestingly, there is evidence that depicts the alternative as being possibly more common (i.e. organisations choose not to communicate talent status to individuals) (Dries & De Gieter, 2014; Björkman et al., 2013). For example, Björkman et al.'s (2013) study, which asked individuals to self-report if they had been identified as a talent or not, saw the largest category being employees citing that they did not know if they had been identified as a talent or not. Similarly, Dries and De Gieter (2014) found that less than 10 per cent of organisations disclosed information about high-potential programmes to staff, and where it was done tended to be on an informal basis.

The often-articulated reason for this, and which has some empirical support, is that the transparency will lead to increased expectations and complacency amongst such individuals. This organisational approach, however, appears somewhat paradoxical in that by failing to disclose talent status, it runs against a key assumption of talent management in terms of differentiation and motivating and retaining the best staff. Ehrnrooth et al.'s (2018) study is informative here in that they reported the transparent communication of talent status does appear to raise expectations. However, while fearful of raising expectations, a failure to do so leads to the question, why bother to undertake talent management?

Based on 24 interviews with individuals identified as 'talent' alongside those evaluated as 'B players' working within the context of a Finnish subsidiary of a large US MNC, Sumelius et al. (2020) examined the impact of communication, or more specifically the absence thereof, on talent status. Acknowledging the wider country culture context whereby exclusive talent management practices sit uncomfortably in Finnish organisations because of the country's egalitarian values, the study found different effects of talent status communication on individuals. The context of intentional 'strategic ambiguity' – deliberately maintaining information asymmetry about who is talent – impacted the conceptualisation, implementation and effectiveness of talent management within the case organisation. Talented individuals, while noting positive feelings from formal communication of their talent status initially, transitioned to ambiguity as they made sense of the implications on the psychological nature of the exchange contract over time. B players, the interviews revealed, were aware of their talent status despite the absence of formal communication. Strategic ambiguity appeared to amplify, rather than compress, negative reactions, with non-talented individuals saying that 'being the last to know' further increased disappointment and negativity. Considering the impact of organisational and country-based discourses further enhances our understanding of ongoing tensions and decision points. It does this by suggesting that egalitarian contexts in which distributive justice is emphasised can complicate endeavours to segment the workforce via talent identification. Notwithstanding the absence of evidence of any long-term positive effects in communicating talent status, the authors ask organisations to be clear in communicating talent pool inclusion and the implications of gaining talent status. Ambiguous and vague communication may risk causing frustration in the very individuals the organisation is seeking to develop and retain. Asplund (2020) also advocates for transparency and openly informing employees of their talent status while also noting that the egalitarian assumptions of 'teachers' can influence the positive outcomes associated with identifying talent and those of classical talent management.

The role of talent management practices

The emerging evidence indicates that if one seeks to realise benefits from talent management, conferring one with such a label or status may be insufficient without implementing or offering appropriate practices, inducements and opportunities. Yet, we know even less about the impact of specific talent management *practices* on talents. A particular issue here and which relates to the ambiguity of meaning, as highlighted in Chapter 2, is that there is no consistency and much diversity in how researchers conceptualise and operationalise talent management practices (Dries, 2013). Similarly, there appears little justification provided by researchers on why they have selected and focused on particular talent management practices over others (De Boeck, Meyers & Dries, 2018). The challenge is that talent management is not a specific practice "but is actually a multi-level construct consisting of distinct, hierarchically ordered components" (De Boeck et al., 2018, p. 201). The De Boeck et al. (2018) systematic review identified 14 empirical and eight non-empirical papers that consider employee reactions or perceptions of talent management practices. In addition, nine non-empirical papers that speak about TM systems, which are dominated by talk of HR practice alignment, were identified. This review unsurprisingly suggests that the type of talent management practice, and how it is measured, is important in the results that will emerge on the outcomes that may be found for how individuals react. Specifically, these authors highlight that positive correlation effects emerge for employee-centric practices (e.g. managerial commitment), but more strategic practices (e.g. talent acquisition, workforce planning) did not provide for statistically significant correlations. Overall, it is surmised that the existing evidence points towards some positive affective, behavioural and cognitive effects of talent management practices. The effect sizes are, however, less than what would often be purported in the talent management literature.

Table 6.2 Key empirical papers on outcomes arising from talent management practices

Reference	Type of study	Key findings
Khoreva et al. (2017)	Quantitative	Stemming from psychological contract fulfilment; the more that talents perceived the effectiveness of talent management practices the greater their commitment to developing leadership competences.
		Female high potentials displayed greater perceptions of talent management practice effectiveness and in turn were more committed to leadership development competence.
Luna-Arocas and Morley (2015)	Quantitative	By developing and institutionalising a talent management system, job performance can be indirectly affected through increasing job satisfaction.
Sonnenberg et al. (2014)	Quantitative	Talent management practices are positively related to psychological contract fulfilment.

Talent management and organisational outcomes

Chapter 1 outlined some of the multiple contributory factors behind the rise of talent management. One reason is arguably magnified to others and may strongly explain the continued interest in talent management practice and research, namely, a belief by organisational leaders that talent management positively impacts organisational outcomes. While there are many industry and professional-type reports and publications that cite the positive and significant relationship between talent management and organisational performance (e.g. Ernst & Young, 2010), there is little by way of scholarly research that corroborates this. Caution is required in respect to the many claims that set out such direct relationships because many of these pieces do not appear to be able to make claims on causation (also an important point that needs to be considered at the individual talent level). There is a danger that assumptions are made too easily of direct linkages between talent management and organisational performance when, as evident in the previous section, this is a much more complex and nuanced matter. This is all the more apparent given the discussion in earlier chapters (see Chapter 2 and 3) on the lack of consensus over the conceptual boundaries of talent management, which in turn will shape the ability to determine the relationship to organisational outcomes.

The complexity involved in realising organisational performance from talent management is nicely exemplified through the Ability, Motivation, Opportunity (AMO) theoretical framework which intimates the importance of HR and talent systems and practices (Boxall & Purcell, 2011). Specifically, while talents may possess the necessary abilities, organisations need to ensure that their practices motivate these individuals and that appropriate developmental opportunities are provided so as to promote and enable strong performance levels. The link between talent management and organisational-level outcomes is therefore more likely to be an indirect relationship with the organisational commitment and individual motivation of talents. However, as noted previously, there is nothing simple in such relationships with context vital in understanding any resultant outcomes.

Scholars such as Boudreau and Ramstad (2005) have spoken about the *potential* for talent management to lead to stronger organisational performance if this involved more systematic and accurate talent decisions. Organisations appear, however, somewhat limited in the development of strong talent management systems underpinned by analytics and data. As such, managerial instinct and with that all the associated biases tend to be the more common situation. It is through more data- and evidence-driven analytical approaches that organisations may better determine the impact of their actions on organisational performance. There is also a clear need for talent researchers to turn their attention to such matters.

In Chapter 2, the idea of staffing an organisation with top performers or A players was introduced as a perspective adopted by some in how they conceptualise talent management. The assumption is that organisational performance is simply the sum of individual performance (Pfeffer, 2001). The reality is, however, much different. Talent is just one part of the equation, and there is an important balancing act and interplay of the individual versus the team dynamic that must be considered. An overly individual talent focus may backfire and reduce the performance levels of individuals, teams and organisations (Beechler & Woodward, 2009). While we understand that a small number of individuals drive much organisational performance, these high performers are inevitably dependent in various ways on colleagues who undertake complementary tasks, roles and functions (Groysberg, 2010). There also needs to be greater recognition and appreciation that not all employees are interested in climbing up the organisational ladder, nor would an organisation want this in reality, and that without solid and competent performers, organisations will not survive.

In essence, there is a need to be very cautious of talent management leading to "the cult of the individual" (Dundon & Rafferty, 2018, p. 382). This is reinforced by studies that question the portability of talent. Groysberg (2010) found that, while the highest performing individuals believed they heavily control their performance levels independent of any organisation, this was not borne out with evidence. For example, their analysis found that when these talents left for another firm, performance levels dropped by up to 20 per cent on average, and it often took up to five years for a return to the pre-move performance levels. Consequently, there is need for caution in how organisations enact talent management, especially where highly exclusive or elitist approaches are adopted. There is also a need to be cautious of being too focused on limited performance measures with insufficient attention being given to the relationships and dynamics of the workplace and employee wellness and welfare issues (Dundon & Rafferty, 2018; Tansley, Kirk & Tietze, 2013).

Conclusion

We can see from the extant literature that the widespread popularity of talent management amongst organisational leaders has not translated into an especially strong body of academic evidence that demonstrates a clear relationship to positive outcomes at individual and organisational levels.

At the individual level, the evidence is mixed, with positive effects emerging but perhaps at smaller margins than may be assumed (De Boeck et al., 2018). Perhaps of most concern are the studies that have identified negative effects. These studies are fewer and less evident in the talent management discourse, which needs redressing. There remain legitimate concerns in respect to the possible erosion of positive effects on the minority (i.e. talents) owing to the undermining of the morale of the majority (i.e. those not in receipt of talent status designation). The relationship between talent management and organisational performance has received scant empirical attention beyond the more consultancy focused reports that make somewhat overly grand claims. In addition, academics may have been somewhat complicit in utilising the seductive discourse in these reports to justify the importance of this field of research. We suggest that there is much relevance with the HR-performance literature (e.g.) whereby there is a need to untangle the 'black box' to better understand the nature of the relationship. The talent management-performance relationship may, however, be an even more complex arena given the varying degrees of workforce differentiation and exclusivity/inclusivity involved. This appears an area ripe for empirical enquiry

Overall, the literature that investigates the impact of talent management can be described as surprisingly sparse for what has been such a burgeoning research domain in the past decade (De Boeck et al., 2018).

References

Asplund, K. (2020). When profession trumps potential: The moderating role of professional identification in employees' reactions to talent management, *The International Journal of Human Resource Management*, 31: 539–561.

Beechler, S. & Woodward, I. C. (2009). The global "war for talent", *Journal of International Management*, 15: 273–285.

Björkman, I., Ehrnrooth, M., Mäkelä, K., Smale, A. & Sumelius, J. (2013). Talent or not? Employee reactions to talent identification, *Human Resource Management*, 52: 195–214.

Blau, P. M. (1964). *Exchange and Power in Social Life*, New York: Wiley.

Boudreau, J. & Ramstad, P. M. (2005). Talent, talent segmentation and sustainability: A new decision science paradigm for a new HR paradigm, *Human Resource Management*, 44: 129–136.

Boxall, P. & Purcell, J. (2011). *Strategy and Human Resource Management*, Third edition, Basingstoke: Palgrave Macmillan.

Cappelli, P. & Keller, J. R. (2014). Talent management: Conceptual approaches and practical challenges, *Annual Review of Organizational Psychology and Organizational Behavior*, 1: 305–331.

Collings, D. G. & Mellahi, K. (2009). Strategic talent management: A review and research agenda, *Human Resource Management Review*, 19: 304–313.

Cropanzano, R. & Mitchell, M. S. (2005). Social exchange theory: An interdisciplinary review, *Journal of Management*, 31: 874–900.

Daubner-Siva, D., Ybema, S., Vinkenburg, C. J. & Beech, N. (2018). The talent paradox: Talent management as a mixed blessing, *Journal of Organizational Ethnography*, 7: 74–86.

De Boeck, G., Meyers, M. C. & Dries, N. (2018). Employee reactions to talent management: Assumptions versus evidence, *Journal of Organizational Behavior*, 39: 199–213.

Dries, N. (2013). The psychology of talent management: A review and research agenda, *Human Resource Management Review*, 23: 272–285.

Dries, N. & De Gieter, S. (2014). Information asymmetry in high potential programs: A potential risk for psychological contract breach, *Personnel Review*, 43: 136–162.

Dundon, T. & Rafferty, A. (2018). The (potential) demise of HRM? *Human Resource Management Journal*, 28: 377–391.

Ehrnrooth, M., Björkman, I., Mäkelä, K., Smale, A., Sumelius, J., & Taimitarha, S. (2018). Talent responses to talent status awareness – Not a question of simple reciprocation, *Human Resource Management Journal*, 28: 443–461.

Ernst & Young (2010). *Managing Today's Global Workforce: Evaluating Talent Management to Improve Business*, London: Ernst and Young.

Festing, M., Kornau, A. & Schäfer, L. (2015). Think talent – Think male? A comparative case study analysis of gender inclusion in talent management practices in the German media industry, *The International Journal of Human Resource Management*, 26: 707–732.

Festing, M. & Schäfer, L. (2014). Generational challenges to talent management: A framework for talent retention based on the psychological-contract perspective, *Journal of World Business*, 49(2), 262–271.

Garavan, T. N. (2012). Global talent management in science-based firms: An exploratory investigation of the pharmaceutical industry during a global downturn, *International Journal of Human Resource Management*, 23: 2428–2449.

Gelens, J., Dries, N., Hofmans, J. & Pepermans, R. (2013). The role of perceived organisational justice in shaping the outcomes of talent management: A research agenda, *Human Resource Management Review*, 23: 341–353.

Gelens, J., Hofmans, J., Dries, N. & Pepermans, R. (2014). Talent management and organisational justice: Employee reactions to high potential identification, *Human Resource Management Journal*, 24: 159–175.

Groysberg, B. (2010). *Chasing Stars: The Myth of Talent and the Portability of Performance*, Princeton, NJ: Princeton University Press.

Höglund, M. (2012). Quid pro quo? Examining talent management through the lens of psychological contracts, *Personnel Review*, 41: 126–142.

Khoreva, V., Vaiman, V. & Van Zalk, M. (2017). Talent management practice effectiveness: investigating employee perspective, *Employee Relations*, 39: 19–33.

Kirk, S. (2020). Sticks and stones: The naming of global talent, *Work, Employment and Society*. https://doi.org/10.1177/0950017020922337

Lacey, M. Y. & Groves, K. (2014). Talent management collides with corporate social responsibility: Creation of inadvertent hypocrisy, *Journal of Management Development*, 33: 399–409.

Luna-Arocas, R. & Morley, M. J. (2015). Talent management, talent mindset competency and job performance: the mediating role of job satisfaction, *European Journal of International Management*, 9: 28–51.

Marchington, M. (2015). Human resource management (HRM): Too busy looking up to see where it is going longer term? *Human Resource Management Review*, 25: 176–187.

Marescaux, E., De Winne, S. & Sels, L. (2013). HR practices and affective organisational commitment: (When) does HR differentiation pay off? *Human Resource Management Journal*, 23: 329–345.

McClean, E. & Collins, C. (2011). High-commitment HR practices, employee effort, and firm performance: Investigating the effects of HR practices across employee groups within professional services firms, *Human Resource Management*, 50: 341–363.

McDonnell, A., Collings, D. G., Mellahi, K. & Schuler, R. S. (2017). Talent management: A systematic review and future research agenda, *European Journal of International Management*, 11: 86–128.

O'Connor, E. P. & Crowley-Henry, M. (2019). Exploring the relationship between exclusive talent management, perceived organisational justice and employee engagement: Bridging the literature, *Journal of Business Ethics*, 156: 903–917.

Pfeffer, J. (2001). Fighting the war for talent is hazardous to your organisation's health, *Organizational Dynamics*, 29: 248–259.

Ready, D., Conger, J. & Hill, L. (2010). Are you a high potential? *Harvard Business Review*, June.

Seopa, N., Wocke, A. & Leeds, C. (2015). The impact on the psychological contract of differentiating employees into talent pools, *Career Development International*, 20: 717–732.

Sonnenberg, M., van Zijderveld, V. & Brinks, M. (2014). The role of talent-perception incongruence in effective talent management, *Journal of World Business*, 49: 272–280.

Sparrow, P. R. & Makram, H. (2015). What is the value of talent management? Building value-driven processes within a talent management architecture, *Human Resource Management Review*, 25: 249–263.

Strauss, A. L. (2017). *Mirrors and Masks: The Search for Identity*, London: Routledge.

Sumelius, J., Smale, A. & Yamao, S. (2020). Mixed signals: Employee reactions to talent status communication amidst strategic ambiguity, *The International Journal of Human Resource Management*, 31: 511–538.

Swailes, S. (2013). The ethics of talent management, *Business Ethics: A European Review*, 22: 32–46.

Swailes, S. & Blackburn, M. (2016). Employee reactions to talent pool membership, *Employee Relations*, 38: 112–128.

Tansley, C., Kirk, S. & Tietze, S. (2013). The currency of talent management – A reply to talent management and the relevance of context: Towards a pluralistic approach, *Human Resource Management Review*, 23: 337–340.

Tansley, C. & Tietze, S. (2013). Rites of passage through talent management progression stages: An identity perspective, *The International Journal of Human Resource Management*, 24: 1799–1815.

7 Talent management and the future of work

A research agenda

Introduction

Talent management has become firmly enshrined as one of the most important and debated ideas within management practice over the past 20 years. The literature and community of scholars undertaking research in this domain have grown exponentially during this period. The preceding chapters have seen us discuss some of the most significant areas of published research on talent management, and in so doing we provided an overarching view on how far this field has travelled in a couple of decades. We suggest that, just like any relatively new and burgeoning research field, there remain limitations and gaps across many domains. For example, advances are still needed in the use of stronger research designs and methodologies, there is much scope to further the quality of conceptual and theoretical development and there are many research questions that still need to be addressed. However, our knowledge and understanding are evolving with each passing year as research endeavours increase in both quality and quantity. As a result, we urge some caution in overly pessimistic evaluations of the field given its recent heritage.

In this final chapter, we turn to the future and, more specifically, what we see as some of the most pertinent areas that future researchers should consider more closely that will help advance knowledge. This research agenda is not meant as exhaustive but instead is focused around advancing the most concentrated areas of talent management research as considered in earlier chapters, along with adding a future work lens to the talent management domain.

Key chapter take-aways

- More critical consideration of the role names, language and meanings take in the literature are necessary.
- Given how the literature has to date treated the term 'talent' and how talent management suffers from a consistency in measurement, there is a danger that not all studies are studying the same phenomenon.

- There is a need to consider the role of time to a greater extent across the talent management divide.
- A more pluralist approach to talent management research and outcomes that emanate from different approaches is encouraged.
- The future of work raises several new domains that need scholarly attention and empirical work ranging from the role of digitalisation and technological innovations to new working arrangements (e.g. the rise of the gig economy).
- The quality of research design and methodological approaches needs to be improved with greater rigour and relevance important.
- The field will ultimately benefit from both enhanced theoretical and methodological plurality.

The role of names, language and meanings in talent management

In Chapters 2 and 3 we discussed the key perspectives or approaches that dominate the literature in terms of defining and conceptualising talent and talent management. There has been much debate around the inadequacies of such conceptualisations, and concerns have been legitimately raised over the loaded nature of the binary categorisation or labelling of people as talents and non-talents. We contend that the importance of language and terminology in talent management deserves further scholarly attention. There is arguably too much inferred by organisations and scholars in what talent is purported to mean. Even where the same terms are used, there is a danger in assuming that there is consistency and conformity in the underlying meanings. These concerns become all the more evident when we know that a substantial proportion of papers fail to even set out what they take to mean by talent and talent management (McDonnell, Collings, Mellahi & Schuler, 2017; Thunnissen & Gallardo-Gallardo, 2019). As such we argue that there is a need for more in-depth studies that consider what these key concepts actually mean. Building on the arguments we make elsewhere (see Wiblen & McDonnell, 2020), we suggest that greater attention should be placed on whether the talk about talent amongst different stakeholders means the same or different things.

We propose that one means which may be an especially fruitful way in which to consider the role of language, names and meanings in talent management is to look to the work of discourse scholars (e.g. Alvesson & Karreman, 2000; Grant & Marshak, 2011). In particular, we point to five non-hierarchical and interrelated levels of talent management-related discourses (see Table 7.1) which merit attention and could offer assistance in advancing our understanding of the nuances and paradoxes associated with

Table 7.1 Levels of talent management-based discourses

Level	Description	Talent management application	Factors to consider	Research aim
Intrapsychic or internal context	The internal thought patterns and dialogues including the internalised stories and introjected beliefs that an individual tells themselves.	Consideration of talent management at the intrapsychic level recognises that we, as individuals, rely heavily on psychological language in making sense of ourselves and others. Our internal scripts, frames and metaphors we use for sensemaking influence how we socially interact, both inside and outside of workplaces. Cognitive frames and schemas both influence and are influenced or shaped by discourses operating at other levels.	The intrapsychic level could include consideration of mental maps, epistemologies, ontologies, motivation and psychological factors associated with the psychology of specific individuals.	The aim is to generate insights into the 'what' and 'why' of mindsets, thinking patterns and internal dialogue of a particular individual.
Individual context	Focuses on the details of the language and words used of and by specific individuals.	Consideration of talent management at the individual level recognises that we, as individuals, deploy specific language, phrases and words to communicate our thinking and understanding of phenomena. Individual discourses both influence and are influenced or shaped by discourses operating at other levels. Individuals' discourses are also shaped by actions.	The individual level could include consideration of the words stakeholders use – or do not use – to refer to talent-based meanings, practices and subjects and the meanings or inferences underpinning individual discourses.	The aim is to generate insights into the 'what' and 'why' of how specific individuals talk about talent management within the context of operational and strategic imperatives.

(Continued)

Table 7.1 (Continued)

Level	Description	Talent management application	Factors to consider	Research aim
Interpersonal and localised context	Focuses on the language and word use of specific groups of individuals at the interpersonal and localised level. Interpersonal and group-based discourses will shape the language, actions and behaviours of individuals in a localised context.	Consideration of talent management at this level recognises that groups of individuals have specific language and words that are used to communicate shared or contested meanings.	This level includes consideration of the language, word use, behaviours and actions between individuals (interpersonal) and within specific teams or specific contexts. This level also includes consideration of how interpersonal and localised discourses shape social order in the everyday conduct of individuals who regularly interact with each other.	The aim is to generate insights into the 'what', and 'why' of language use between individuals or within groups of individuals. The aim is to also understand how the what and the why of language use shapes social actions and behaviours – the 'where' and 'what' of talent management.
Organisational context	Focuses on the accumulation and aggregation of language and word use at the interpersonal and localised context-level discourses and social interactions in organisations. Interactions at the interpersonal and localised context level will shape and influence organisational discourses and actions.	Consideration of talent management at this level recognises that organisations do not exist in and of themselves. Rather organisations are the aggregation of individuals and groups of individuals. There is the potential for certain interpersonal and localized-level discourses to feature prominently in organisational discourses, while other discourses do not.	The organisational level includes consideration of how (and to what extent) language and words used in specific interpersonal and localised contexts influence discourses within and between organisations. The organisational level also includes consideration of how (and to what extent) behaviours and actions enacted within specific interpersonal and localised contexts feature within and between organisations.	The aim is to understand 'how', 'what', and 'why' certain language and word use features within organisational discourses while others do not. The aim is to also understand 'how', 'where', 'what' and 'why' certain behaviours and actions feature within organisations while others do not.

| Societal, institutional and phenomenological context | Focuses on the discourses which feature at the broader societal level and across institutional domains. | Consideration of talent management at this level recognises that meanings, practices and subjects arise within a larger set of systems operating within specific social groups, institutions and/or understandings of the premises and possibilities directing an industry or organisational sector. | This level includes consideration of how (and to what extent) recognised, embedded, historical language and word use within broader domains, including societies, countries, industries (places/locations), influence talent management meanings and practices.

It includes consideration of how (and to what extent) existing and broader knowledge of particular phenomena shape and influence social interactions and accepted behaviours. | The aim is to understand the larger picture associated with talent management and to recognise how all discourse levels interact with broader contexts and understandings to establish accepted ways of knowing and acting. |

talent management. We suggest that consideration of the operation of talent and talent management at different levels may well provide an opportunity to advance our understanding of this multilevel phenomena. This, in turn, may offer one possible mechanism for future theory generation that will help address some existing concerns in this regard.

More particularly, this table identifies several research aims depending on the level one wishes to consider the specific talent management discourses. For example, in the societal, institutional and phenomenological context, research could be undertaken that better understands the bigger picture associated with and which influences talent management. At an organisational level, the focus may be on seeking to understand how, what and why particular language and words feature in the organisational discourse and become dominant over other alternatives.

We finish this section by posing an especially provocative question: is the term 'talent' useful? When one considers the widespread meaning, both implicitly and explicitly, that is evident across the literature, along with the potential issues and problems that may arise, it forces us to ask: how much benefit is garnered by its continued use? There is a real danger, given how the field currently treats this term, that scholars may not actually be studying the same phenomenon. In reviewing the evidence around the outcomes arising from the conferring of talent status in Chapter 6, we learnt that a more complex equation appears to exist than the early studies (e.g. Björkman, Ehrnrooth, Mäkelä, Smale & Sumelius, 2013; Swailes & Blackburn, 2016) indicated. It is argued that talent status may have a moderation rather than direct motivational effect on individual reactions (Ehrnrooth et al., 2018). However, given the limitations highlighted with how the term talent has been evaluated in the literature, there is a real need for caution in making overly strong determinations on what this body of research can and cannot say. Basically, is everyone talking about the same thing?

We believe that there is a need for scholarly discourse to engage with the utility of the term and determine whether perhaps the use of more longstanding terms such as 'high potentials', 'high performers', and 'stars' may be more effective for future research advancement as they provide more delineated measures (though they are also not without issues). To date, it can be argued that talent has become more like a catch-all term than offering more fine-grained clarity on meaning. As there can be substantial variation in how the term is treated within organisations, the regular calls for greater clarity on how one is defining the term may ultimately prove a pointless exercise.

Talent management practices and outcomes

Our discussion of talent identification highlighted how scholars seek to offer prescriptive and normative assumptions about how organisations could or should identify talent. Most scholars argue that systematic approaches – whereby criteria and processes are predefined and consistently applied – are likely to be most effective (Berger & Berger, 2003; Collings & Mellahi, 2009; Jooss, Burbach & Ruël, 2019a; Mellahi & Collings, 2010). A systematic approach rather should decipher which specific individuals or groups of individuals possess the defining characteristics of a talented subject. The goal, whether articulated or implied, is to identify individuals of greater value, when compared relative with their peers. Despite the emphasis on workforce differentiation as a core differentiating factor, many scholars fail to acknowledge that talent determinations, when conducted systematically, compare notions of high performance and high potential within a bounded context (i.e. team/function and organisation level). Talent management research has thus far been quiet on how best to consider how determinations of individual performance, potential and talent can be appropriately considered, and appreciate the wider contextual factors at play. This is an important area that requires attention, especially as the direct effects of talent management are increasingly questioned (Ehrnrooth et al., 2018).

Debates and discussions about the 'how' of talent identification are fraught with complexity. Empirical studies of talent management continuously find that organisations do not have overly systematic approaches in place (Jones, Whitaker, Seet & Parkin, 2012; Mäkelä, Björkman & Ehrnrooth, 2010; Wiblen, 2016; Wiblen, Dery & Grant, 2012). The desire to have one way or a consistent way is debated within organisational boundaries with evidence that decisions may be best achieved through a two-stage process which includes relevant stakeholders (see Chapter 4), as a group, talking about the value of individuals to ensure some degree of consensus about who gains talent pool admission. Moreover, we also know that there are long-standing issues and concerns with how organisations evaluate performance (Ellis & Saunier, 2004), something that is fraught with less difficulty than arriving at valid and reliable forms of evaluating potential.

Complexity will ensue because the practice asks stakeholders to share their opinions about how specific individuals have performed their talent. Talent as a performative construct, whereby individuals are evaluated on how they performed, underpins this practice. Talent identification in practice, therefore, is arguably less about criteria and process per se, but rather how relevant stakeholders perceive how individuals applied their talent within specific contexts, tasks and activities. Talent identification also involves stakeholders judging those actions and reflecting on whether they mirrored expectations and the strategic needs of the manager, team/ function and/or organisation. While scholars can profess the inadequacy of basing talent determinations on the gut-feel or intuition of evaluators, there is evidence that illustrates that many are identified this way. Rhetoric around talented individuals having the 'right stuff' (Dries, 2013; Ready, Hill & Conger, 2009; Swailes, 2013), or assertions that 'I know talent when I see it' (Wiblen, 2016; Wiblen et al., 2012) gives rise to the need to engage with how intuitive evaluations occur. While one may simply dismiss intuition, we encourage researchers to engage with the 'how' and 'what' of such approaches to understand what factors and variables influence talent status and how this may affect talent pool composition.

There is also a need for more critical engagement with the debates about performance and potential when talking about talent identification. Existing conceptualisations of talent as referring to high potential typically fail to address the key question – how does one identify potential in an objective, reliable and valid manner? Potential for what? Potential is ultimately a more latent-styled factor in that it is not readily observable given it is not yet realised and more a precondition of future success and achievement; this may see it viewed in an innate way (Altman, 1997; Yost & Chang, 2009). The measurement of potential therefore takes on some importance. It tends to often be seen as one's capacity and ability for further growth, such as to be promoted at least two levels above one's existing role. Given changing organisational structures to flatter, matrix forms this type of approach would seem somewhat limited as a way of considering potential. Overall, we would benefit from learning more about the basis for these judgments and how resulting decisions fare.

The idea of timing is something that has received insufficient attention in the context of talent management practice. Specifically, to what extent is talent identification a point-in-time exercise or a dynamic process? We have seen stories right across the sporting divide in terms of individuals who arrive late to become a star. This is worthwhile to consider in the context of organisational talent management. For example, are organisations able to, and how do they, take account of the possible 'late-bloomer'? Staying with the concept of time, there is also the other side; if one has been designated as a talent, is that something that they hold 'for life' or is it more fluid, whereby individuals move in and out of talent pools? This has received little to no consideration both conceptually and empirically in the literature. Sumelius, Smale and Yamao (2020) noted that while there were often feelings of pride and happiness, sense of achievement and increased self-esteem from being a talent, these same individuals had no awareness of the duration this lasted, nor what was expected in terms of maintaining it. This leads to natural follow-up questions: what impact does it have on an individual to lose talent status? Under what conditions or circumstances does this take place? Also, are there cases whereby someone loses it but regains it in future years, and how does this play out? These are important questions that merit critical enquiry to help inform better practice.

Overall, we call on and encourage researchers to broaden the current talent management research agenda. While we agree that the study of specific talent management practices is under-represented in the current literature (McDonnell et al., 2017; Thunnissen, Boselie & Fruytier, 2013), there is a need to shift the boundaries somewhat to focus more on the entire process, rather than just on discrete events, activities or practices. There is also a need to widen what practices are focused on, given how Chapter 5 noted that, notwithstanding the normative and prescriptive assumptions about the various resources talent could, should and do access, there has been a significant oversight in respect to research that examines how organisations develop talent. Moreover, other key talent management practice areas have also received limited consideration, such as the differential rewards and benefits approaches for those in receipt of talent status.

Such matters are important in considering what impact or influence talent management has on outcomes across different levels of analysis (e.g. individual, team, organisational). While, Chapter 6 noted that there appears to be emergent evidence of positive individual outcomes arising from talent status and being in receipt of differentiated investment, opportunities and practices, it was also flagged that a negative side may exist. Overall, there is a need for increased research activity on the impact of talent management and for this to also incorporate possible negative outcomes. In so doing, we would gain greater appreciation of the extent to which talent status and talent management may be a double-edged sword for individuals and organisations. This, in turn, will enable greater understanding of how to facilitate the more positive effects.

While the more popular theoretical approaches (e.g. social network theory, psychological contract theory) are useful, there is also scope to draw from additional perspectives here to help unpack the tensions and paradoxes that exist for individuals. For example, Kirk (2020) offers a refreshingly alternative perspective through socio-onomastics to reveal the challenges faced by talents in balancing the positive (e.g. increased developmental opportunities) with less positive aspects (e.g. increased expectations, workload). There is a need for more critical and pluralist lenses to be applied in talent management studies (Dundon & Rafferty, 2018) if we are to truly advance knowledge and understanding around the merits of this strategic management activity that appears to be taking hold across organisational life. There is a need for caution amongst both practitioners and scholars to not make too many assumptions on the positive effect of talent management without sufficient delineation of possible negative dimensions both for talents and those excluded from such pools or programmes. In this regard, the applicability of ethical and sustainability theories may offer utility in bringing a more holistic appreciation of the wider context within which talent decisions exist and the impacts and outcomes that may arise.

The future of work and talent management

Imagine the future of work by considering the following talent management practices: a future worker applies for a job without a resume or curriculum vitae; machine learning identifies and reaches out to passive candidates rather than recruiters; an employee is hired without being interviewed by a person; companies abolish their annual performance appraisal system; employees enjoy unlimited vacation and discretionary paid time off; email is considered passé as a work communication tool; an algorithm predicts who is likely to leave your company soon; customized employee benefits are paying off student loans or helping with employee transitions; and questions for an HR generalist are answered by a chatbot.

(Claus, 2019, pp. 207–208)

This quote encapsulates what some may see as blue-sky thinking, while others may view it as the inevitability of the changing nature of work due in no small part to rapid technological advancements and disruptions. While only time will tell us whether Claus' (2019) imagination takes hold, there is no doubt that the future of work is a key influence and impact on talent management. There is an array of fascinating and worthwhile research avenues that are deserving of scholarly enquiry and comment. We focus on two aspects, namely, the role of technology and digitalisation, and what the rise of the gig economy means for talent management.

The increasing role of technology and digitalisation in the world of work and talent management

Information technology has a role in managing talent. Boudreau and Ramstad (2005) have suggested technology may increase HR managers' ability to improve talent. However, the scale of importance of this role within organisations may range from pivotal and central to minimalist and non-existent. Whether part of an enterprise planning system, human resource information system or specialist digital talent management system, technology options offer organisations a mechanism to appropriate talent management systems and a tool to manage the much-cited systematic approach to talent identification and management. Numerous compelling reasons support the increased use of technology in talent management, including:

- to enable greater consistency in identifying talent across the organisation (Stahl et al., 2007) and establish the employees that organisations want to especially develop and retain (Lah & Capperella, 2009).
- to enable greater incorporation of time and longitudinal analysis.
- to forecast supply and demand for current and future talent pools through a unified and accessible talent database (Snell, 2008).
- to improve decision-making (Lengnick-Hall & Moritz, 2003) by providing and producing information that can establish linkages between human capital assets and the performance of the business; and produce dynamic, real-time metrics, analytics and data about an organisation's human capital assets and hence 'talent' (Williams, 2009).

Technology vendors (e.g. SAP, Oracle, Workday) provide organisations with the abilities and workflow processes that enable assessment of an individual's performance and potential. That is, technology can dictate the how of talent management through facilitating systematic and consistent evaluation where all individuals are allocated numerical scores. Some senior stakeholders assert that talent can be identified by using technology, whereby the embedded algorithms that are primarily vendor designed rank all individuals (Wiblen & Marler, 2019). Such rankings from the highest performer or with the highest potential to the lowest performer and those with lower potential underpin talent lists. In its most simplistic form, senior executives may then decide to arbitrarily decide on a specific proportion (percentage) of the workforce to be deemed talent and accordingly allocated to the internal talent pool.

Vendors claim that technology facilitates faster and more accurate decision-making and gives organisations access to best practices. However, there is a need for greater critical consideration of this. In this vein, we call for caution against the vendor rhetoric inferring that information systems-based approaches underpin effective talent management. This is even more important in what we see as a context of increased influence amongst vendor-designed talent management. There needs to be more deliberate reflection on the role of digitalisation and the various technologies that are used in managing internal talent and strategic workforce planning. While we argue that there is limited debate about the salience of controlling costs, increasing use of digitalised talent management results in vendors playing a pivotal role in the design of talent management systems, the identification of talent as per the predetermined criteria (including skills and capabilities) and processes for talent pool formation. These companies own the infrastructure, which means that they shape and amend, update and reconfigure the software largely on their deciding. Control over improvements and innovations, such as amendments to codes, criteria, algorithms and workflow processes remains with the vendor. While organisations can update and reconfigure the system, each customisation brings additional costs (both financial and time). There is the potential, therefore, that organisations outsource talent criteria and identification processes to external and removed third parties. This leads us to the question: to what extent is there alignment between technologically enabled frameworks and strategic organisational outcomes? This may mean that organisations are not getting what they want or need fully in terms of being aligned with their own organisational context and strategy (see Chapter 2). Are organisations too easily buying into the sales pitch by these software vendors claiming 'leading' and 'best practice' packages will bring effective talent management? Before engaging in any such digital investment, organisations need to be very clear on what they want from talent management and how it relates to their own strategic objectives.

Organisations are increasingly looking at talent-based decisions occurring automatically with little to no human intervention. When electing to automate talent decisions or aspects of talent management practice, organisations must still decide *how* (original emphasis) to automate (Jesuthasan & Boudreau, 2018). Decisions about automation require identifying the different kinds of automation and garnering an informed understanding of their applicability. Framing questions about the value of automation within the context of operational and strategic needs is essential. Jesuthasan and Boudreau (2018) encourages scholars and practitioners alike of the need to acknowledge that frameworks underpinning automation require constant management and evaluation. There is potential that it will enable more stringent analysis to inform decisions by enabling greater inputs into decision-making. However, the use of automation should not be a decide-and-then-forget approach. Rather, automation requires continuous surveillance. The advent of automation means that talent management will become a more iterative process where there is no clear beginning or end. Talent management will therefore become a complex adaptive system that continually evolves. Understanding talent management in the era of increasing digitalisation and automation requires an informed understanding of both the technology and the practices in place. Siloed knowledge generation will not suffice in the context of this era of technological innovations, but more inter- and transdisciplinary perspectives will be required.

There needs to be greater debates about who (i.e. humans or technology) should be tasked with talent management. This is becoming more amplified a domain as technological innovations promise so much. Researchers can help organisations work through what talent management and HRM processes may benefit from automation and those which best require human intervention and agency. Moreover, it is understanding the complex interaction between the two that is especially important in unpacking in future studies.

Expanding the contextual boundaries of talent management: the rise of gig work

The focus of talent management research has unsurprisingly been very focused on more traditional industries and organisational forms. However, we have witnessed the emergence of the gig or platform economy, which can be defined as an economic system that utilises online platforms to digitally connect individuals with clients and consumers (Todolí-Signes, 2017) and which to some represents one of the greatest economic changes in recent years (Kenney & Zysman, 2016). Gig work can be argued as representing a profound shift from traditional, human-centred management within organisational boundaries, towards a more self-management approach that is enabled by technology and which falls outside how we tend to conceptualise an organisation (Duggan, Sherman, Carbery & McDonnell, 2020). As such, the gig economy represents a domain that will give rise to different talent issues (Kirven, 2018). While the extent to which the gig economy will take hold is very much open to question, we are witnessing a not-insignificant proportion of people deciding to embark upon some type of gig or freelance work. The gig economy offers organisations great possibilities of accessing a wider and more global talent pool for specific tasks or roles they need undertaken. However, Mandloi (2020) points to a reluctance amongst many organisations to make much use of gig workers, which may be due to uncertainty on how to best incorporate them within traditional organisational life and structures. For example, how does the organisation incorporate gig workers with permanent staff to create cohesive teams? How does it enable appropriate knowledge transfer and engagement? How does it manage both side by side?

At a surface level, the gig economy appears especially welcome by the younger working population who seek enhanced work-life balance. In saying that, we know very little about how this working life will leave individuals across their lifespan. For example, what does a career mean for the gig worker? Are they solely responsible for self-career management and training and development, and how does this play out over time? Kost, Fieseler and Wong's (2020), provocation paper debates the possibilities of boundaryless careers in the gig economy. They, however, note that while the gig economy appears to offer fertile conditions for such career development, the reality may be somewhat different with several significant issues that provide some hindrance. Moreover, there is a need for consideration of the different types of gig work (Duggan et al., 2020). For example, in the context of careers and work, those gig workers undertaking more high-skills tasks "may experience greater psychological mobility and agency, and they may have a much easier time finding work beyond the gig economy, provided that they are proactive", compared to those in lower end work (Kost et al., 2020, p. 102).

Taking a more critical and negative perspective, gig work also represents an especially precarious working situation which could deprive substantial numbers of people globally of any sort of employment security, which may lead to significant wider impacts from the capacity to purchase their own house, lack of pensions, social benefits and so forth. In effect, the gig economy offers a different way of viewing and practising work that offers both potential positives and drawbacks. What is very evident is that existing legislation, HR systems and talent management programmes are designed on the more traditional employment model (Cascio & Boudreau, 2016). Without a clear employment relationship between the gig worker and either the platform organisation or the consumer of the task, there are clear question marks over the applicability and underpinning assumptions around HR and talent systems from recruitment to training and development to compensation (Meijerink & Keegan, 2019). As a result, there is a fundamental question as to what role talent management may play in the gig economy. Do any of the talent management ideals, as discussed in this book, apply to gig work?

The rise of the gig economy also speaks to the previous section on digitalisation in that here the interaction of both human and technology actors is without question. Talent management in the gig economy involves a different set, or enhanced role, of actors in the form of greater customer or requester involvement, alongside the critical role of the algorithm. What should the talent management value proposition look like in the context of these working arrangements? What might a talent management architecture look like that enables customisation according to specific types of workers? Is this viewed as relevant in the context of gig work given they tend to be viewed as independent contractors rather than employees? While there is some evidence of platform firms providing some degree of investment in their freelancers, the opposite (i.e. little to no responsibility for supporting the development of talent) is likely to be more common (Rosenblat & Stark, 2016; McKeown, 2016).

Research design and methodology: a call for improved rigour

Much of this book has focused on reviewing the extant talent management literature with the aim of providing a succinct overview of the key themes that have gained the most consideration in the field, along with deciphering a future research agenda in this final chapter. In addition to considering content areas and key research questions to be addressed, it is important to consider research design and methodology in the context of moving the field forward. Notwithstanding the clear increase in scholarly research over the past two decades in this field, it is important to also consider the quality of the underpinning data on which the field is based. In short, there are substantial concerns in respect to both rigour and relevance of talent management scholarship. Amongst the key methodological issues raised in Thunnissen and Gallardo-Gallardo's (2019, pp. 175–177) systematic review were "carelessness in defining core concepts", "lack of transparency regarding research methodology", "untraceable and misleading respondents", "fuzzy research designs" and being "loosely embedded in context".

These concerns are important to raise, and scholars must be aware of the negative impact this will cause if not addressed in future research. Overall, there is a considerable need for more sophisticated and high-quality research designs if the field can be expected to progress. Without appropriate rigour, then there is also a lack of relevance of such studies (Vermeulen, 2005). Given this situation, there is not only a responsibility on us as scholars to continue to improve the research design and methodologies employed but also to raise appropriate questions when reviewing such work for potential publication. A failure to do so is likely to accentuate the fragmentation of the field only further (Antonakis, 2017; Sparrow, 2019). Many of the aforementioned concerns can be addressed in relatively straightforward ways, such as ensuring sufficient detail is provided in papers on the research design employed. However, there is also a need for a more fundamental rethink amongst researchers in terms of how studies are designed to ensure there is appropriate rigour and relevance to their work. For example, it is critical that scholars are explicit on how they have measured key concepts to provide confidence that conclusions can be drawn on the phenomenon of interest.

Quantitative work appears more common but tends to remain at the more descriptive and cross-sectional level and with a heavy focus on senior organisational respondents. Consequently, we call on those undertaking talent management research to be more ambitious in the design of studies. For example, there is a need for more multilevel and longitudinal approaches. While these are more challenging, resource-intensive and time-consuming to undertake, they also confer the potential for significant advances in knowledge and impact. Moreover, there is scope to employ more high-quality, qualitative approaches in our research, depending on the question we are seeking to address. Greater use of observation, ethnography, discourse analysis and design thinking are all likely to offer more pluralistic perspectives that we argue can only assist with the advancement of understanding and knowledge. We strongly encourage not only greater theoretical plurality but methodological plurality in this burgeoning field of academic research.

Conclusion

Ultimately, talent management scholarship has come a long way in a relatively short space of time. It is important that due recognition is given to the considerable research activity that has taken hold and which has been central in building debate amongst scholars and practitioners on what business see as a critical strategic management activity. Notwithstanding this, there is also a need for the community of scholars to take a step back and evaluate where the field is going, acknowledge the limitations that exist within our current knowledge base, including conceptual and theoretical understanding, alongside issues around rigour and relevance.

While there may be some who believe debates around the definitions and parameters of the field's most central concepts are becoming tiresome, we suggest differently. These foundational elements remain in need of more critical consideration alongside far more rigorous empirical work. This chapter could not possibly cover all worthy future research areas; rather we have focused on what we see as especially important in the context of the existent state of knowledge while also factoring in especially pertinent current trends and issues around digitalisation and new forms of working.

References

Altman, Y. (1997). The high-potential fast-flying achiever: Themes from the English language literature 1976–1995, *Career Development International*, 2: 324–330.
Alvesson, M. & Karreman, D. (2000). Varieties of discourse: On the study of organisations through discourse analysis, *Human Relations*, 53: 1125–1149.
Antonakis, J. (2017). On doing better science: From thrill of discovery to policy implications, *Leadership Quarterly*, 28: 5–21.
Berger, L. & Berger, D. (Eds.). (2003). *The Talent Management Handbook: Creating a Sustainable Competitive Advantage by Selecting, Developing and Promoting the Best People*, New York: McGraw-Hill Professional.
Björkman, I., Ehrnrooth, M., Mäkelä, K., Smale, A. & Sumelius, J. (2013). Talent or not? Employee reactions to talent identification, *Human Resource Management*, 52: 195–214.

Boudreau, J. W. & Ramstad, P. M. (2005). Where's your pivotal talent? *Harvard Business Review*, 83: 23–24.

Cascio, W. & Boudreau, J. (2016). The search for global competence: From international HR to talent management, *Journal of World Business*, 51: 103–114.

Claus, L. (2019). HR disruption – Time already to reinvent talent management, *Business Research Quarterly*, 22: 207–215.

Collings, D. G. & Mellahi, K. (2009). Strategic talent management: A review and research agenda, *Human Resource Management Review*, 19: 304–313.

Dries, N. (2013). The psychology of talent management: A review and research agenda, *Human Resource Management Review*, 23: 272–285.

Duggan, J., Sherman, U., Carbery, R. & McDonnell, A. (2020). Algorithmic management and app-work in the gig economy: A research agenda for employment relations and HRM, *Human Resource Management Journal*, 30: 114–132.

Dundon, T. & Rafferty, A. (2018). The (potential) demise of HRM? *Human Resource Management Journal*, 28: 377–391.

Ehrnrooth, M., Björkman, I., Mäkelä, K., Smale, A., Sumelius, J. & Taimitarha, S. (2018). Talent responses to talent status awareness – Not a question of simple reciprocation, *Human Resource Management Journal*, 28: 443–461.

Ellis, C. M. & Saunier, A. M. (2004). Performance appraisal: Myth and reality, in L. A. Berger & D. R. Berger (Eds.), *The Talent Management Handbook: Creating Organizational Excellence by Identifying, Developing and Promoting Your Best People*, New York: McGraw-Hill.

Grant, D. & Marshak, R. J. (2011). Toward a discourse-centered understanding of organizational change, *The Journal of Applied Behavioral Science*, 47: 204–235.

Jesuthasan, R. & Boudreau, J. (2018). *Reinventing Jobs: A 4-step Approach for Applying Automation to Work*, Boston, MA: Harvard Business Review Press.

Jones, J. T., Whitaker, M., Seet, P.-S. & Parkin, J. (2012). Talent management in practice in Australia: Individualistic or strategic? An exploratory study, *Asia Pacific Journal of Human Resources*, 50: 399–420.

Jooss, S., Burbach, R. & Ruël, H. (2019a). Examining talent pools as a core talent management practice in multinational corporations, *The International Journal of Human Resource Management*, 1–32. https://doi.org/10.1080/09585192.2019.1579748

Kenney, M. & Zysman, J. (2016). The rise of the platform economy, *Issues in Science and Technology*, 32: 61–69.

Kirk, S. (2020). Sticks and stones: The naming of global talent, *Work, Employment and Society*. https://doi.org/10.1177/0950017020922337

Kirven, A. (2018). Whose gig is it anyway? Technological change, workplace control and supervision, and workers' rights in the gig economy, *University of Colorado Law Review*, 89: 249–292.

Kost, D., Fieseler, C. & Wong, S. I. (2020). Boundaryless careers in the gig economy: An oxymoron? *Human Resource Management Journal*, 30: 100–113.

Lah, T. E. & Capperella, J. (2009). Using talent supply chain management to overcome challenges in the professional services market, *Workforce Management*, 88(3).

Lengnick-Hall, M. & Moritz, S. (2003). The impact of e-HR on the human resource management function, *Journal of Labor Research*, 24: 365–379.

Mäkelä, K., Björkman, I. & Ehrnrooth, M. (2010). How do MNCs establish their talent pools? Influences on individuals' likelihood of being labeled as talent, *Journal of World Business*, 45: 134–142.

Mandloi, R. (2020). Making the most of talent in the gig economy, *Harvard Business Review Blog*, 13 January. Retrieved from: www.harvardbusiness.org/making-the-most-of-talent-in-the-gig-economy/

McDonnell, A., Collings, D. G., Mellahi, K. & Schuler, R. (2017). Talent management: A systematic review and future prospects, *European Journal of International Management*, 11: 86–128.

McKeown, T. (2016). A consilience framework: Revealing hidden features of the independent contractor, *Journal of Management & Organization*, 22: 779–796.

Meijerink, J. & Keegan, A. (2019). Conceptualizing human resource management in the gig economy: Toward a platform ecosystem perspective, *Journal of Managerial Psychology*, 34: 214–232.

Mellahi, K. & Collings, D. G. (2010). The barriers to effective global talent management: The example of corporate élites in MNEs, *Journal of World Business*, 45: 143–149.

Ready, D. A., Hill, L. A. & Conger, J. A. (2009). Winning the race for talent in emerging markets, *Harvard Business Review*, 87: 117–117.

Rosenblat, A. & Stark, L. (2016). Algorithmic labor and information asymmetries: A case study of Uber's drivers, *International Journal of Communication*, 10: 3758–3784.

Snell, A. (2008). The future of talent management, *Workforce Management*, 87(20).

Sparrow, P. (2019). A historical analysis of critiques in the talent management debate, *BRQ Business Research Quarterly*, 22: 160–170.

Stahl, G., Björkman, I., Farndale, E., Morris, S. S., Paauwe, J., Stiles, P. & Wright, P. M. (2007). Global talent management: How leading multinationals build and sustain their talent pipeline, *INSEAD Working Papers Collection*, 34: 1–36.

Sumelius, J., Smale, A. & Yamao, S. (2020). Mixed signals: Employee reactions to talent status communication amidst strategic ambiguity, *The International Journal of Human Resource Management*, 31: 511–538.

Swailes, S. (2013). The ethics of talent management, *Business Ethics: A European Review*, 22: 32–46.

Swailes, S. & Blackburn, M. (2016). Employee reactions to talent pool membership, *Employee Relations*, 38: 112–128.

Thunnissen, M., Boselie, P. & Fruytier, B. (2013). A review of talent management: "Infancy or adolescence?", *The International Journal of Human Resource Management*, 24: 1744–1761.

Thunnissen, M. & Gallardo-Gallardo, E. (2019). Rigor and relevance in empirical TM research: Key issues and challenges, *BRQ Business Research Quarterly*, 22: 171–180.

Todolí-Signes, A. (2017). The gig economy: Employee, self-employed or the need for a special employment regulation? *Transfer: European Review of Labour and Research*, 23: 193–205.

Vermeulen, F. (2005). On rigor and relevance: Fostering dialectic progress in management research, *Academy of Management Journal*, 48: 978–982.

Wiblen, S. (2016). Framing the usefulness of eHRM in talent management: A case study of talent identification in a professional services firm, *Canadian Journal of Administrative Sciences*, 33: 95–107.

Wiblen, S., Dery, K. & Grant, D. (2012). Do you see what I see? The role of technology in talent identification, *Asia Pacific Journal of Human Resources*, 50: 421–438.

Wiblen, S. & Marler, J. H. (2019). The human – Technology interface in talent management and the implications for HRM, in R. Bissola & B. Imperatori (Eds.), *HRM 4.0 for Human-Centered Organisations*, Brigley, UK: Emerald Publishing Limited, pp. 99–116.

Wiblen, S. & McDonnell, A. (2020). Connecting "talent" meanings and multi-level context: A discursive approach, *The International Journal of Human Resource Management*, 31: 474–510.

Williams, H. (2009). Job analysis and HR planning, in M. Thite & M. J. Kavanagh (Eds.), *Human Resource Information Systems. Basics, Applications, and Future Directions*, Thousand Oaks, CA: SAGE Publications, pp. 251–276.

Yost, P. & Chang, G. (2009). Everyone is equal, but some are more equal than others, *Industrial and Organizational Psychology*, 2: 442–445.

Index

Note: Page numbers in **bold** indicate a table on the corresponding page.

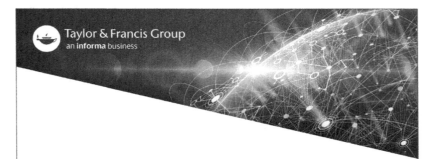

Printed in the United States
by Baker & Taylor Publisher Services